test your
Smarts

THE BIG BOOK OF
SELF-SCORING IQ TESTS

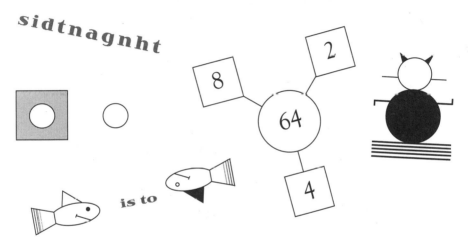

sidtnagnht

is to

Donatella Bergamino
and
Marina Raffo

Sterling Publishing Co., Inc.
New York

Graphic design: Donatella Bergamino, Marina Raffo, Francesca Chiapponi
Translated by John Foster
Edited by Claire Bazinet

Library of Congress Cataloging-in-Publication Data Available

10 9 8 7 6 5 4 3 2

Published by Sterling Publishing Company, Inc.
387 Park Avenue South, New York, N.Y. 10016
English translation and revisions © 2001 by Sterling Publishing Co., Inc.
Originally published in Italy under the title *Nuovi Test
di Intelligenza* by L.I.BER Progetti Editoriali
© 1998 by The Twin Brothers
Distributed in Canada by Sterling Publishing
c/o Canadian Manda Group, One Atlantic Avenue, Suite 105
Toronto, Ontario, Canada M6K 3E7
Distributed in Great Britain and Europe by Cassell PLC
Wellington House, 125 Strand, London WC2R 0BB, England
Distributed in Australia by Capricorn Link (Australia) Pty Ltd.
P.O. Box 6651, Baulkham Hills, Business Centre, NSW 2153, Australia

Sterling ISBN 0-8069-5893-6

Contents

Preface

"Am I smart?" Modern psychology suggests that the actual question should be, "Do I have a high IQ?"

Intelligence Quotient tests provide a fairly accurate evaluation of a person's intelligence, and the tests in this book will give the reader a useful indication of his or her IQ. We are not suggesting that these tests assess every possible form of human intelligence, but rather that they provide a means to measure intelligence in certain precise classifications and will permit readers to make a solid validation of their IQ.

Explanations are provided along with the answer keys to help you with questions that you were unable to answer or that you got wrong. Not only will these tests help determine your IQ, but they are also good mind exercises. By taking note of your thought processes as you take the tests and by studying the results, you will gain a better understanding of how your mind works and how to make it work better.

Before You Start

Measuring Intelligence

There are various methods to calculate IQ. Many tests have a standard procedure to calculate the result in terms of deviation and distance (above and below the median). Usually, in this case, the fixed median is 100. Other tests count the number of questions within the test and calculate the IQ by the number of correct responses. The median equals approximately half the number of attempts.

This book measures the score of each of the three most characteristic forms of intelligence, defined by modern psychology as: verbal intelligence, numeric intelligence, and spatial intelligence. There are seven tests incorporating a variety of questions, followed by specific tests for each type of intelligence.

The verbal exam contains questions covering anagrams, knowledge of general culture, word completion, and missing letters. The numerical exam deals with the test taker's ability to calculate, and his or her intuition. The spatial exam only requires good eyesight and attention to detail to determine picture differences.

Taking the Tests

To answer the different types of questions and achieve a valid score:

1. Allow 40 minutes for each test. It may help to have someone, who is not taking the test, time you. If that is not possible, use a stopwatch or timer.
2. Don't allow anyone to disturb you or to help you during the tests.
3. The tests contain questions that you are supposed to think about. Don't look at the questions prior to taking the tests. This will not benefit you or give you a valid score.
4. After finishing one test, wait at least a half hour before taking another. You will be more relaxed and your mind more focused on the upcoming test.
5. Before taking a test, read these instructions to refresh your memory. During the test, take the time to read each question carefully, so as not to waste time on incorrect answers.

Some types of questions included in these tests:

Numeric pattern (find the next number in a series)
Numeric letter pattern (find next in series, using alpha-order values)
Numeric, letter, and verbal analogies (i.e., "is to")
Letter or number finds (complete word or number pattern)
Word anagrams (unscramble and select in/out word)
Spatial test (find next figure in series or that doesn't belong)

Good luck!

IQ TESTS

TEST 1

1) What number best completes the series?

    4   7   10   13   ...

2) Complete the following analogy:

    Man is to masculine as woman is to .....

    (a) girl   (b) feminine   (c) wife   (d) lady

3) What two numbers complete this series?

    8   11   10   9   12   7   6   9

4) Which of the following figures does not belong?

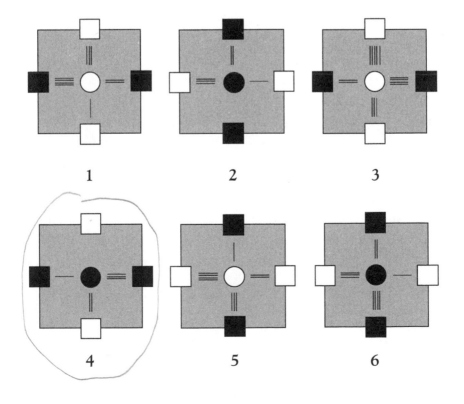

         1   2   3

         4   5   6

5) Which of these word anagrams is not a flower?

piltu

cridoh

nanitraco

nejirup

airadneg

6) What word, added to each initial letter, forms other words?

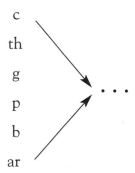

7) What number is missing?

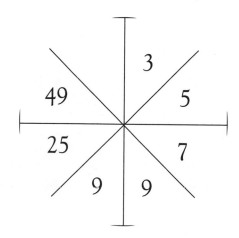

8) **Which of the numbered figures best completes the series?**

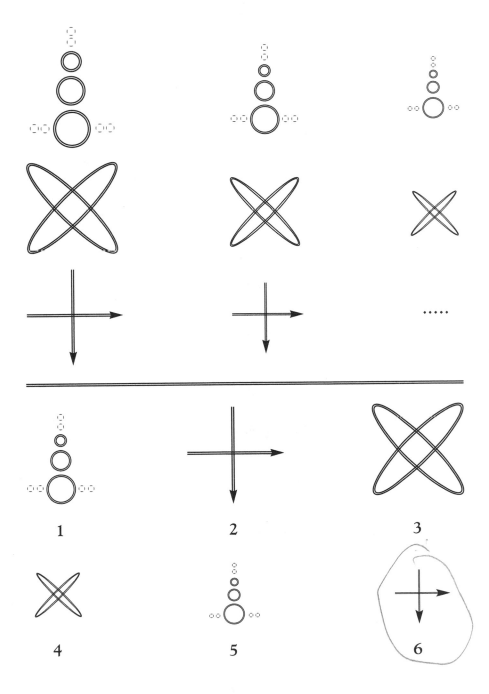

9) What number is missing?

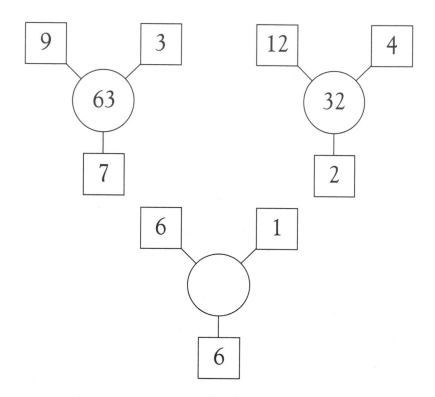

10) Which of the following does not belong?

Paris   New York   Rome   London
Bangkok   New Delhi   Beijing

11) What number is missing?

2   3   4   6   8   10   16   24

12) What letter best completes the series?

j   l   o   s   .....

13) Which of these word anagrams is not a U.S. city?

gronba

inhoxep

toditer

sangvelto

noterlam

dnartolp

14) What is the missing number?

3   6   6

4   9   12

2   3   .....

15) Which of the following figures does not belong?

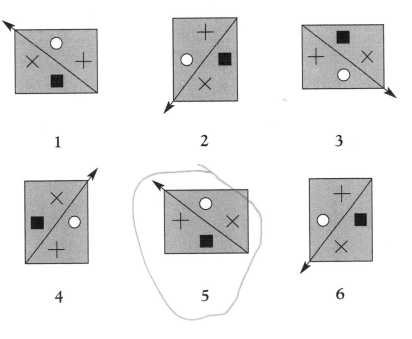

1   2   3

4   5   6

16) What number best completes the series?

    2   3   7   13   27   .....

17) Which of these words does not belong?

    queen   king   pawn   bishop   cardinal   castle

18) What is the missing letter?

c	e	o
a	b	b
b	g	n
f	b	.....

19) What are the missing numbers?

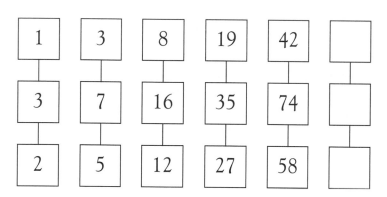

20) Which two words are the most alike?

    (a) match   (b) wheel   (c) hole
    (d) iron   (e) blacksmith   (f) pencil

21) Which of the numbered figures best completes the series?

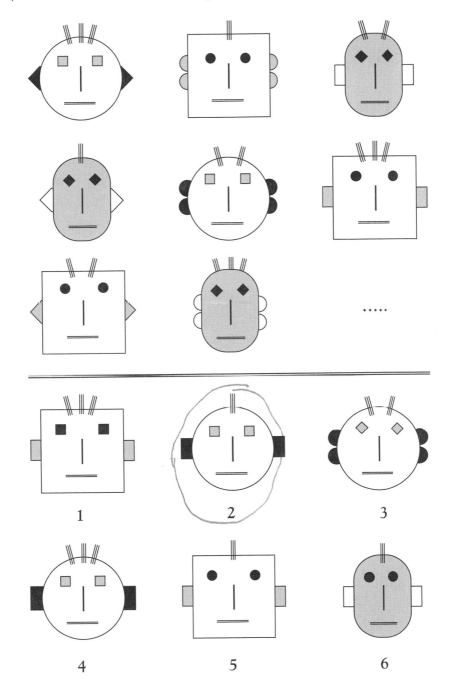

1

2

3

4

5

6

22) Choose the correct answer.

Ashley is bigger than Denise, but not as big as Fran. Sheila, Denise's friend, is shorter than her cousin Adria, but bigger than her sister Fran.

Who is the shortest?

(Ashley, Denise, Fran, Adria, Sheila)

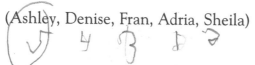

23) What number is missing from the triangle?

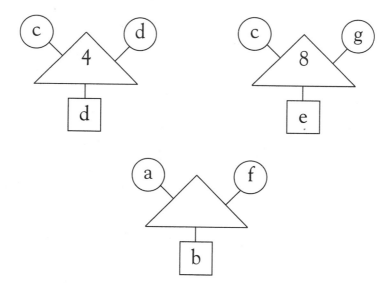

24) Choose the correct statement.

Two parallel lines never intersect.

(a) Is always true   (b) Is never true
(c) Is sometimes true   (d) Is an opinion

25) Which of the numbered figures best completes the series?

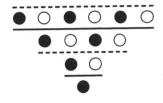 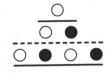

1

2

3

4

5

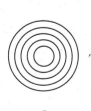

6

26) Complete the following analogy.

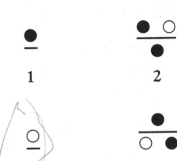 is to as is to

1   2   3   4

27) Which of these word anagrams does not belong?

honyvac

ottru

reghnir

adrisen

ahlew

askhr

28) What are the missing numbers?

27   29   25   33   17   .....

25   23   27   19   35   .....

31   33   29   37   21   .....

29) What word best completes the series?

trombone   clarinet   tuba   oboe   saxophone

(a) tambourine   (b) harp   (c) bassoon   (d) viola

30) What are the missing letters?

a   e   i

d   h   l

g   k   o

....

31) Complete the following analogy.

165135 is to peace as 1215225 is to .....

32) Which of the numbered figures best completes the series?

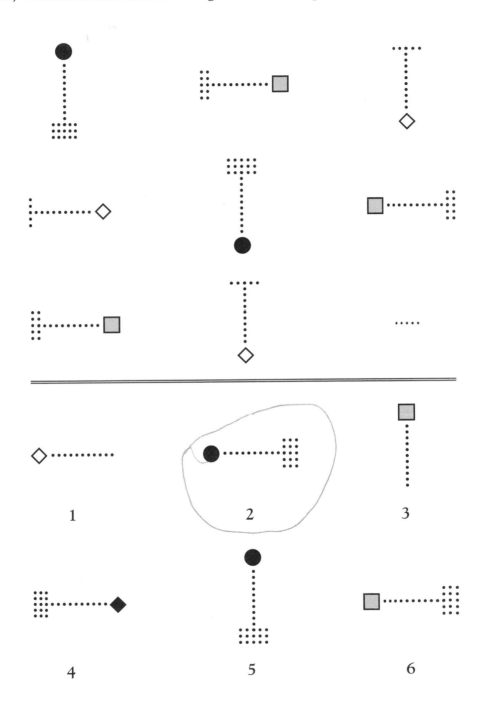

1

2

3

4

5

6

33) What numbers belong in the parentheses?

217 (266) 315

315 (.....) 413

314 (11) 111

213 (.....) 412

175 (16)   95

200 (.....) 125

34) What are the missing letters?

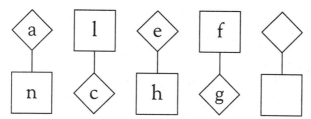

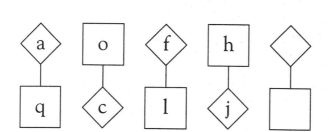

35) What number best completes this series?

6   9   27   54   675   .....

36) Which of the numbered figures best completes the series?

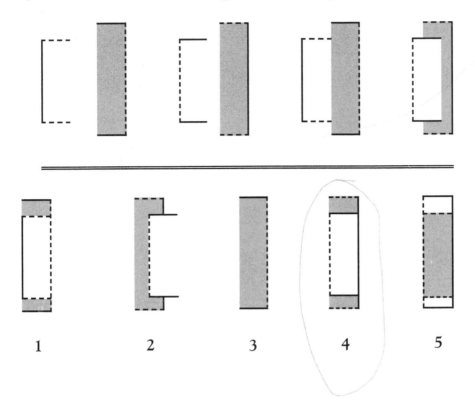

1   2   3   4   5

For test solutions, turn to page 20.

Test 1 Solutions

1) **16.** The numbers increase by 3.

2) **b.** Feminine.

3) **14, 5.** There are 2 alternate patterns: one increasing by 2, one decreasing by 2.

4) **5.** The lines diminish counterclockwise.

5) **juniper.** The other words are: tulip, orchid, carnation, and gardenia.

6) **row.**

7) **81.** The square of the diagonally opposing number.

8) **6.** The figures become smaller from left to right.

9) **12.** Multiply the three numbers in the outside squares and divide the sum by 3.

10) **New York.** It's the only city that is not a capital.

11) **12.** Alternately multiply each number by 2.

12) **x.** The letters progressively skip 1, 2, 3, 4 places.

13) **Montreal.** The other cities are: Bangor, Phoenix, Detroit, Galveston, and Portland.

14) **2.** Multiply the first two numbers and then divide the sum by 3.

15) **5.** In this figure, the cross is with the black box and the x is with the white circle.

16) **53.** Every number is multiplied by 2 and then alternately changed +1, −1.

17) **cardinal.** It is the only choice that is not a chess piece.

18) **l.** Multiply the order values of the first two letters.

19) **89, 153, 121.** Every number is multiplied by 2 and then added to: +1, +2, +3, +4, +5.

20) **b and c.** They both have a circular form.

21) **2.** The three series alternate ears, hair, and eye shapes.

22) **Denise.**

23) **2.** Multiply the letters in the circles, subtract the number in the square, and divide the sum by 2.

24) **a.**

25) **4.** Each figure: reverses, loses a line, and alternates circle colors.

26) **4.**

27) **whale.** It's the only mammal. The other words are: anchovy, trout, herring, sardine, and shark.

28) **49, 3, 53.** Each column across adds +2, –4, +8, –16, +32.

29) **(c) bassoon.** They are all woodwinds.

30) **j, n, r.** The letters skip 3 in the horizontal columns and 2 in the vertical columns.

31) **love.** Uses numerical order of letters.

32) **2.** Each column has three basic types: circle, square, diamond; and 1, 2, and 3 base lines.

33) **364.** Add the two outer sets and then divide by 2.
13. Add all the numerals in the outer sets together.
15. Subtract one outer set by the other and divide by 5.

34) **i, d.** Skip a letter going up the alphabet in the diamond boxes and down a letter in the square boxes.
o, c. The letters go up the alphabet in a 1, 2, 3, 4 series in the diamond boxes and down the alphabet in the square boxes.

35) **2241.** There are two alternate series. Multiply the first number by itself and subtract the sum by the next number.

36) **1.** The outer figure progressively moves towards the shaded figure. The dotted lines change alternately.

TEST 2

1) **Which of these word anagrams does not belong?**

   slotec

   hoccu

   sidtnagnht

   uerabu

   pabrededs

   arhic

2) **What are the missing numbers?**

   2   3   5   8   12   17.

   23   18   14   11   9   6.

   4 – 4 – 3 ~ 3

3) **What word, added to the parentheses, completes one word and starts the second?**

   as (.....) cil

   ma (.....) age

4) **What are the missing letters?**

   c   l   a

   e   n   c

   g   p   e

   ....

5) **Complete the following analogy.**

   Short is to 1811010 as skinny is to .....

6) What numbers belong in the parentheses?

98 (33) 79

23 (.....) 55

12 (26) 13

11 (.....) 6

125 (21) 20

70 (.....) 35

7) What number is missing from the center square?

5	4	1
3	4	3
2	2	6

8) What number best completes the series?

2   8   3   27   4   .....

9) Which of the numbered figures best completes the series?

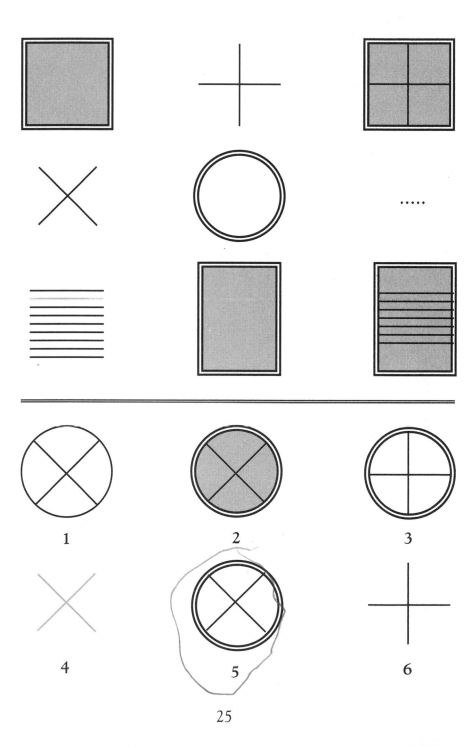

1   2   3

4   5   6

10) Complete the following analogies.

Auto is to steering wheel as bicycle is to .....

(a) wheel   (b) saddle   (c) handlebars   (d) moped

Eye is to sight as nose is to .....

(a) touch   (b) sense   (c) smell   (d) hearing

Chicago is to Illinois as Montreal is to .....

(a) Canada   (b) province   (c) Quebec   (d) Toronto

11) What number is missing from the triangle?

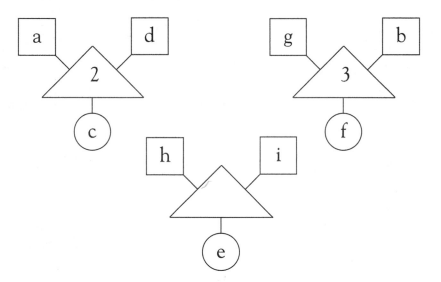

12) Choose the correct statement.

All animals are mammals.

(a) Is always true   (b) Is never true
(c) Is sometimes true   (d) Is an opinion

13) Which numbered figure comes next in the series?

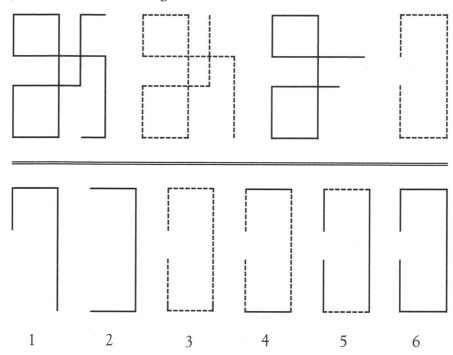

1	2	3	4	5	6

14) Which numbered figure completes the analogy?

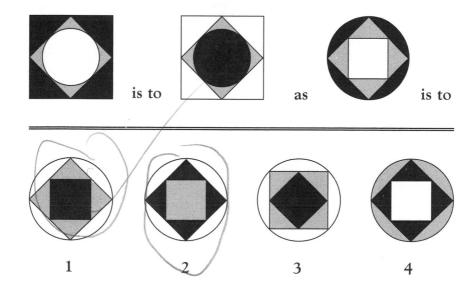

1	2	3	4

27

15) Which of the numbered figures best completes the series?

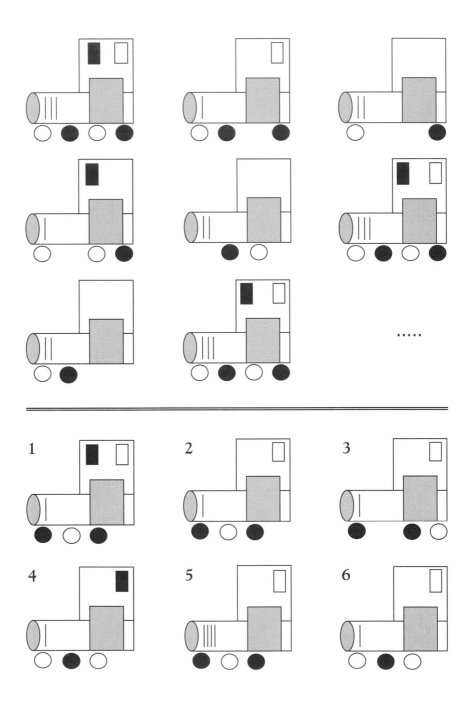

16) What number best completes the series?

3   8   6   11   9   .....

17) Which of the following does not belong?

Oslo   Paris   Rome   Barcelona

Beijing   Frankfurt   Prague

18) Which of the word choices best completes the series?

McKinley   Popocatepetl   Shasta   Rainier   .....

(a) Everest   (b) volcano
(c) Whitney   (d) mountain

19) What are the missing numbers?

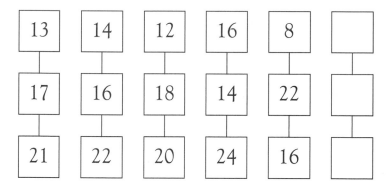

20) Which of the following does not belong?

icicle   nail   cone   fork   horseshoe   arrow

21) Which of these word anagrams is not a sport?

luncigr

bigbacer

roascsel

lwstnrieg

gyubr

ceryarh

22) What word, added to the initial letters, forms other words?

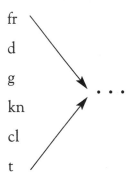

fr

d

g

kn

cl

t

23) What is the missing number?

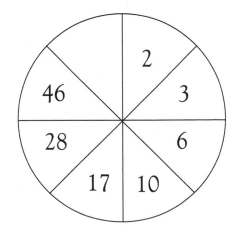

24) What number is missing from the circle?

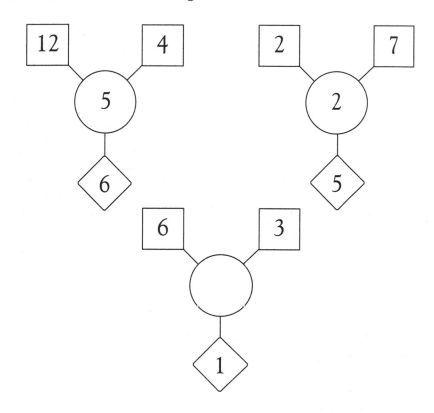

25) Which of these words does not belong?

foot   elbow   head   knee   skull   toe

26) What number best completes the series?

9   12   7   10   5   .....

27) What letter best completes the series?

h   l   o   s   v   .....

28) Which of the numbered figures best completes the series?

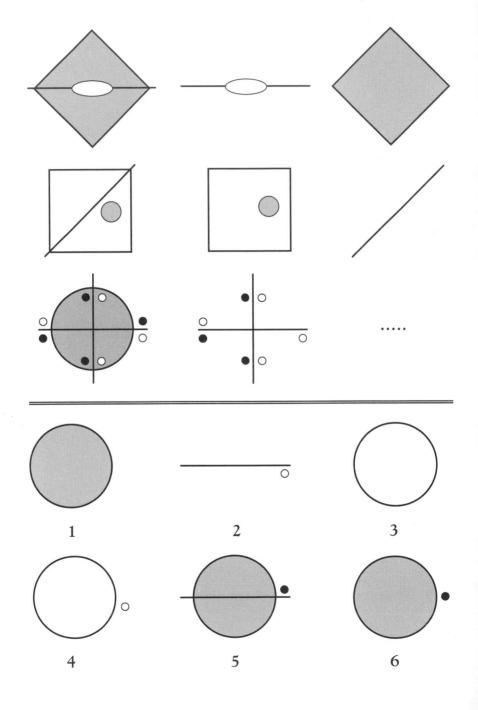

1   2   3

4   5   6

29) **Which of these word anagrams does not belong?**

ibiat

emorfar

emruf

altepal

srumueh

30) **What is the missing number?**

3	2	12
1	4	8
2	4	.....

31) **Which of the following figures does not belong?**

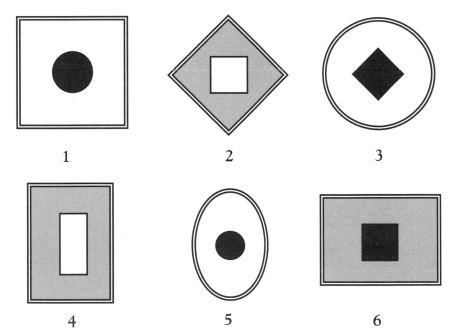

32) What number best completes the series?

1   2   9   .....

33) Complete the following analogy.

Sea is to Mediterranean as island is to .....

(a) Alaska   (b) Cuba   (c) coast   (d) archipelago

34) What number best completes the series?

2   3   3   6   15   .....

35) Which of the following figures does not belong?

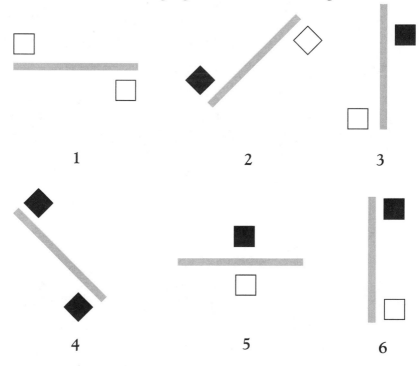

1   2   3

4   5   6

36) Which of the numbered figures best completes the series?

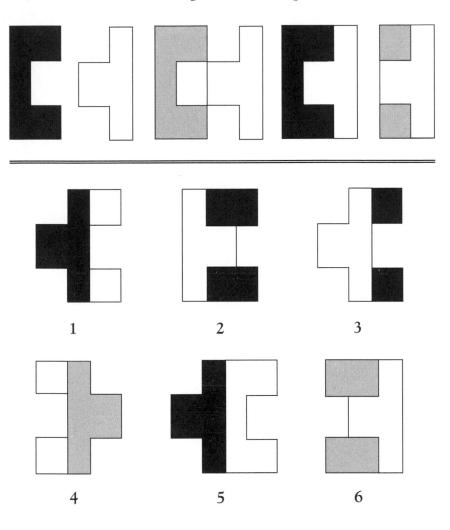

1   2   3

4   5   6

For test solutions, turn to page 36.

Test 2 Solutions

1) **bedspread.** The other words are: closet, couch, nightstand, bureau, chair

2) **17, 8.** The first set of numbers increases by +1, +2, +3, +4, +5. The second set of numbers decreases by –5, –4, –3, –2, –1.

3) **pen, dam.**

4) **i, r, g.** Each series skips a letter.

5) **6120 (fat).** Numerical value of letters.

6) **15.** Add all the single numerals.
   11. Multiply the numbers outside the parentheses and divide the product by 6.
   7. Subtract the numbers outside the parentheses and divide the difference by 5.

7) **4.** The sum of each column is 10.

8) **64.** There are two patterns. The first pattern increases by +1 from the number 2. The second pattern cubes each number in the first pattern.

9) **5.** The figures are added together.

10) **c, c, c.**

11) **12.** Add the numbers in the outside squares and subtract the sum from the circle.

12) **b.**

13) **2.** Two lines are progressively eliminated while also alternating between solid and dotted lines.

14) **1.**

15) **6.** In every figure series, there are 4, 3, 2 circles; 2, 1, 0 windows; and 3, 2, 1 vertical lines.

16) **14.** The pattern alternates between +5 and –2.

17) **Beijing.** It's the only non-European city.

18) **c.** All are names of mountains in North America.

19) **24, 6, 32.** The pattern runs horizontally: +1, –2, +4, –8, +16

20) **horseshoe.** All other choices have points.

21) **cribbage.** It's a card game. The other words are: curling, lacrosse, wrestling, rugby, archery.

22) **own.**

23) **75.** Add the first number and the second number, the second with the third, etc., and add 1 to each sum.

24) **4.** Add the numbers in the outside squares, subtract the sum from the diamond, and divide the sum by 2.

25) **elbow.** It is the only word with two syllables.

26) **8.** The pattern alternates between +3 and −5.

27) **z.** The pattern alternately skips 3 and 2 letters.

28) **6.** Subtract the second figure from the first figure.

29) **forearm.** The others are names of bones: tibia, femur, patella, and humerus.

30) **16.** Multiply the first two numbers and double the product.

31) **4.** It's the only figure with two figures equally combined.

32) **730.** Cube the proceeding number and add +1.

33) **b.**

34) **87.** Multiply the first two numbers and subtract 3 from the product.

35) **6.** It is the only figure that has two squares on one side.

36) **3.** The figure progressively advances. The black and gray alternate.

SELF-SCORING

Less than 14	=	Poor	−
From 15 to 19	=	Adequate	☆
From 20 to 24	=	Fair	☆
From 25 to 29	=	Good	☆☆☆
From 30 to 36	=	Excellent	☆☆☆☆

TEST 3

1) Which of the numbered figures best completes the series?

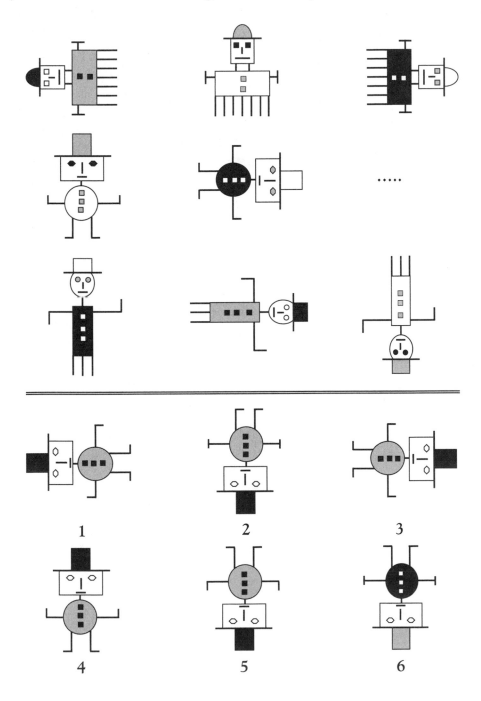

1

2

3

4

5

6

2) What number is missing from the circle?

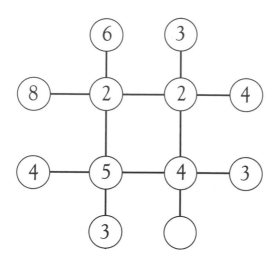

3) What numbers are missing from the squares?

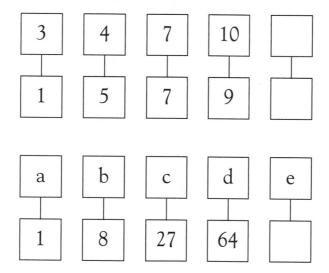

4) What is the next number?

1   4   9   16   25   .....

5) Which of these word anagrams is not a nation?

nazaitan

ambru

rakenmd

natenriag

snaaksar

atsalariu

6) What two letters complete this series?

7) What letters, missing from the parentheses, complete these two words?

ya (...) ge

ze (...) r

8) What is the missing letter?

g	c	c
e	c	e
f	d	c
b	h	.....

9) What is the missing number?

10) Choose the correct answer.

Laura, Sara, Irene, and Monica take seats in the movies in this order. But soon Monica changes seats with Laura, who then changes her seat with Sara. During intermission, Sara decides to leave, so Laura returns to her seat.

Who is sitting on the right-hand side of the group?

(Laura, Sara, Irene, Monica)

Who is sitting by herself?

(Laura, Sara, Irene, Monica)

11) What number is missing from the triangle?

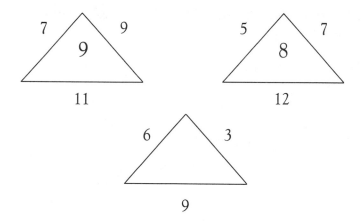

12) Choose the correct statement.

All babies born with green eyes have parents with green eyes.

(a) Is always true   (b) Is never true
(c) Is sometimes true   (d) Is an opinion

13) Which of the numbered figures best completes the series?

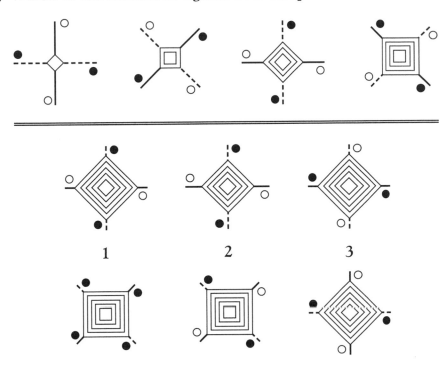

14) Which numbered figure completes the following analogy?

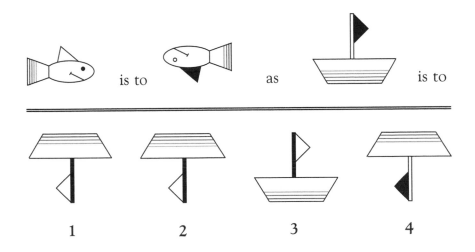

is to   as   is to

43

15) **What number is missing from the circle?**

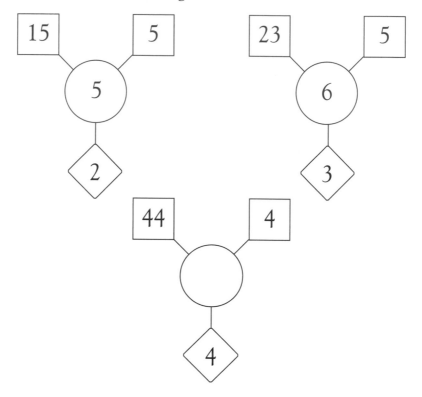

16) **Which of these words does not belong?**

Mars   Jupiter   Orion   Saturn
Neptune   Uranus   Earth

17) **What number best completes the series?**

1   2   1   3   2   7   .....

18) **What letter best completes the series?**

a   d   h   m   .....

19) Complete the following analogy.

Donatella is to 284537115 as natal is to .....

20) Which of the following does not belong?

cylinder   square   cone
cube   rectangle   pyramid

21) Which of the choices best completes the series?

temperas   watercolors   oils   pens   .....

(a) paper   (b) paintbrushes   (c) arts   (d) pencils

22) What number is missing from the center circle?

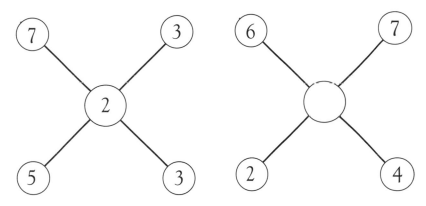

23) Which words are most alike?

(a) while   (b) direction   (c) to go
(d) time   (e) car   (f) always

24) Which of these word anagrams does not belong?

rozmat

icupinc

scpoasi

whiengrs

evdri

25) What is the missing number?

1	3	5
3	4	3
6	3	.....

26) Which of the figures does not belong?

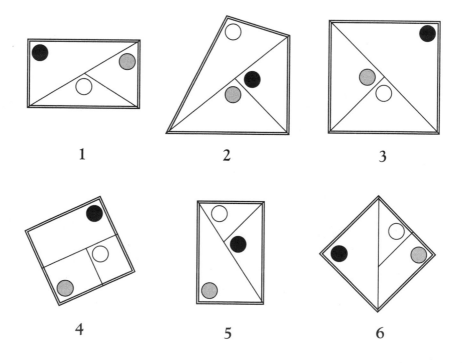

1   2   3

4   5   6

27) Which of the numbered figures best completes the series?

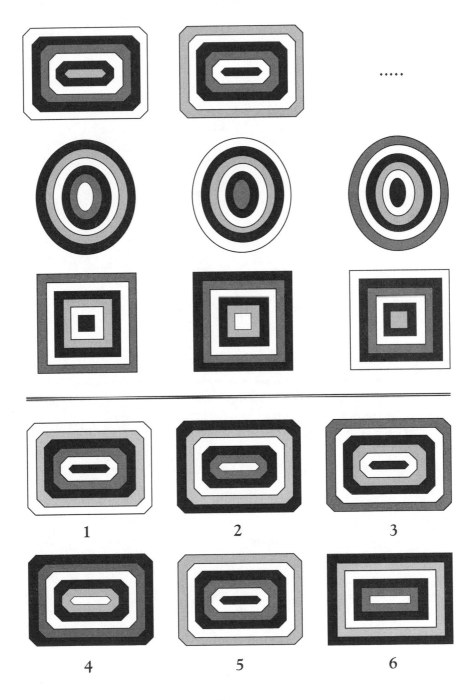

28) Which of the numbered figures best completes the series?

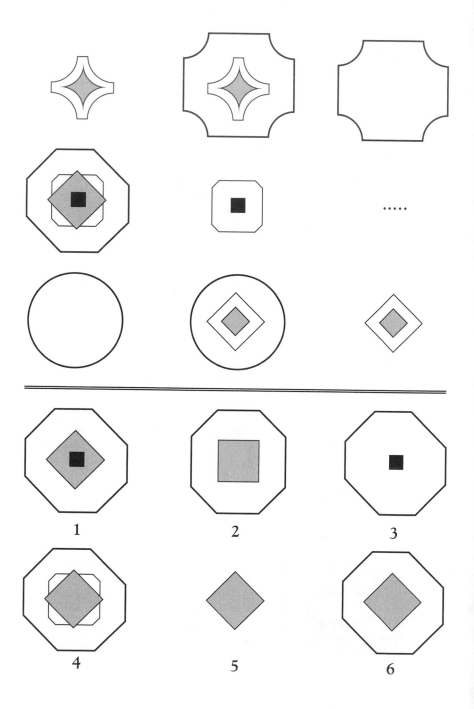

29) Which of these word anagrams does not belong?

phojes

cresanf

etpahisen

beahzietl

aerbrot

acamir

30) What word, added to each initial letter, forms new words?

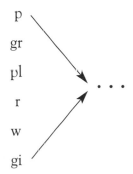

p

gr

pl

r

w

gi

. . .

31) What letters are missing from the sections?

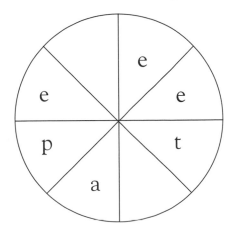

32) What number is missing from the final series?

3   7   5   1   6   8   4   9   .....

33) Complete the following analogy.

Sock is to foot as glove is to .....

(a) arm   (b) wool   (c) hand   (d) body

34) What is the missing number?

3   6   33   .....

35) Which of the following figures does not belong?

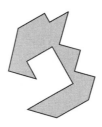

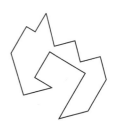

1

2

3

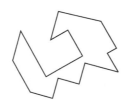

4

5

6

36) Which of the numbered figures is next?

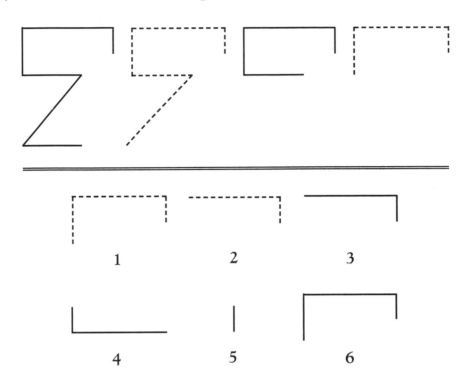

1   2   3

4   5   6

For test solutions, turn to page 52.

Test 3 Solutions

1) **5.** The figure rotates 90 degrees.

2) **7.** The sum of the circles in every line is 16.

3) **11, 13.** There are two patterns. The first diagonally increases by 2 from the top. The second increases diagonally by 3 from the bottom.
125. The number in the bottom square is the cube of the number value of the letter in the upper square.

4) **36.** The pattern progressively increases: +3, +5, +9, +11.

5) **Arkansas.** The other words are: Tanzania, Burma, Denmark, Argentina, Australia.

6) **l, k.** There are two alternating patterns that skip 2 letters.

7) **rda, phy.**

8) **c.** The sum of every row is 13.

9) **25.** There are two alternating series. The first, in the squares, simply increases by 1. The second, in the circles, is the square of each number in the first series.

10) **Laura, Monica.**

11) **6.** Add the numbers in the outside squares and divide the sum by 3.

12) **b.**

13) **6.** The figure rotates 45°, a center square is added, and the circles alternately change between black and white.

14) **1.**

15) **10.** Subtract the numbers in the outside squares and divide the difference by the number in the rhombus.

16) Orion. It's a constellation, not a planet.

17) **13.** Multiply the first numbers and add +1, −1 to their results.

18) **s.** The pattern progressively skips +2, +3, +4, +5 letters.

19) **45351.** Letters are number coded.

20) **Rectangle.** It's the only two-dimensional figure.

21) **d.**

22) **7.** Subtract the sums of the top and bottom circles.

23) **while, always.** They are the only adverbs.

24) **Picasso.** A painter, as opposed to musical composers: Mozart, Puccini, Gershwin, Verdi.

25) **2.** The sums of both columns are 10.

26) **2.** It's the only figure that is not a rectangle.

27) **2.** The shadings progressively succeed each other.

28) **6.** The figures overlap.

29) **Joseph.** The othersJ are feminine names: Frances, Stephanie, Elizabeth, Roberta, and Marcia.

30) **ant.**

31) **r, r.** Forms the word repartee.

32) **2.** The sum of the three groups is 15.

33) **c.** Hand.

34) **1086.** Double each number and subtract by 3.

35) **5.** It's the only figure that's not within 180° counterclockwise.

36) **2.** The figure progressively loses a side.

TEST 4

1) Which of the numbered figures best completes the series?

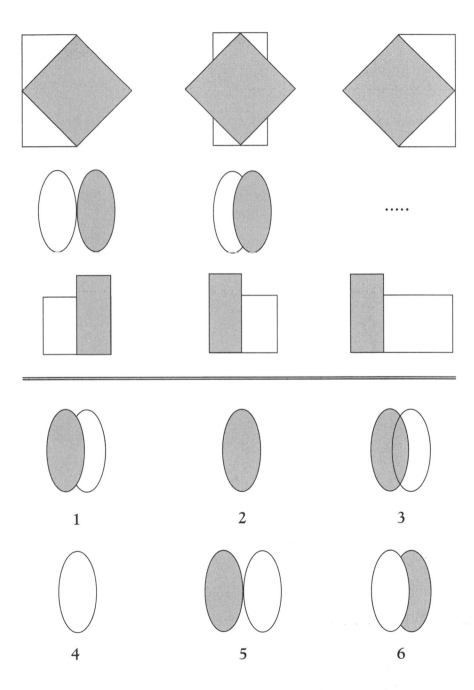

2) What number is missing from the square?

4	12	3
6	4	6
8	6	

3) What number is missing from the base of the figure?

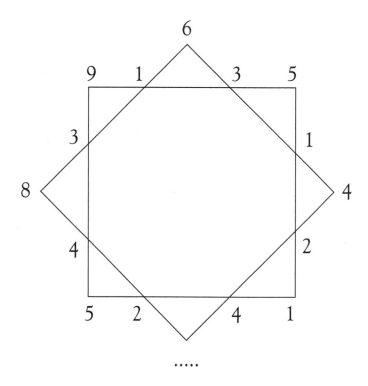

4) What letter comes next in the series?

b   e   i   p   .....

56

5) Which of these word anagrams does not belong?

    chekint

    chuht

    ircdorro

    boharmot

    reofy

6) What is the missing word?

    horse (rope) depot

    valve (....) decal

7) What two related words are spelled out in the series below?

    cpoanvcermeetnet

8) What number is missing from the square?

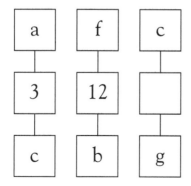

9) Complete the following analogy.

    9 is to 81 as 2 is to .....

10) Choose the correct answer.

Eddie received a higher grade on the final exam than Krista, but not as high as Larry. Lori received a lower grade than her cousin Leanne, but did better than Krista.

Who received the lowest grade?

(Eddie, Krista, Lori, Larry)

11) What number is missing from the square?

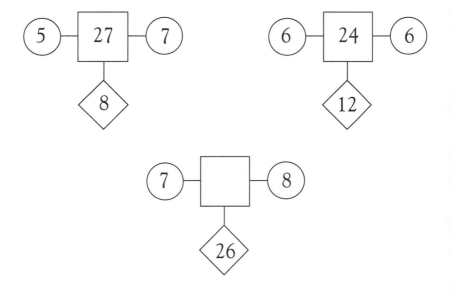

12) Choose the correct statement.

Animals have four legs.

(a) Is always true   (b) Is never true
(c) Is sometimes true   (d) Is an opinion

13) Which of the numbered figures comes next in the series?

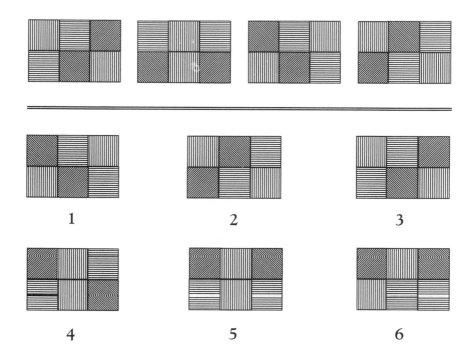

14) Complete the following analogy.

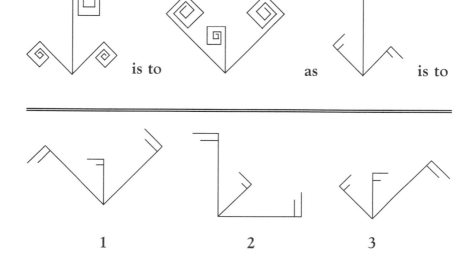

is to ... as ... is to

1   2   3

15) What number is missing from the square?

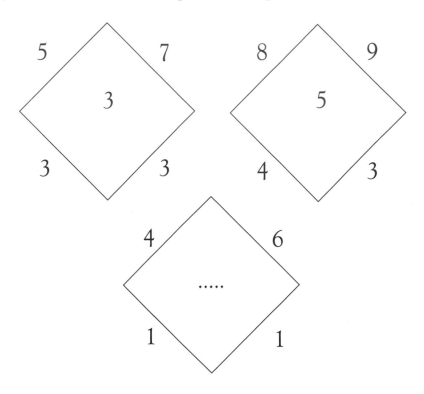

16) Which of these words does not belong?

violet   blue   yellow   azure
sky blue   indigo   green

17) What number best completes the series?

3   2   7   15   106   .....

18) What letter best completes the series?

c   f   h   k   m   .....

19) **Complete the following analogy.**

   5 is to 125 as 7 is to .....

20) **Which of these words does not belong?**

   Poodle   Great Dane   Labrador
   Siamese   Boxer   Airedale

21) **Choose the answer that best completes the series.**

   dollar   mark   franc   peso   .....

   (a) loot   (b) change   (c) ruble   (d) bills

22) **What number is missing from the square?**

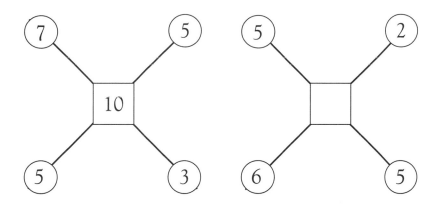

23) **Which one of the following numbers does not belong?**

   124   26   17   1125
   1264   81   144   14

24) Which of these word anagrams does not belong?

lemsl

renaigh

ithgs

rae

setat

25) What is the missing number?

3	2	12
5	3	30
4	2	.....

26) Which of the following figures does not belong?

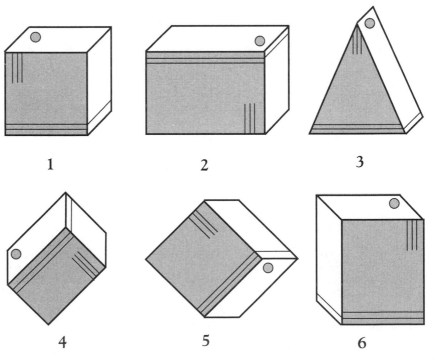

27) Which of the numbered figures best competes the series?

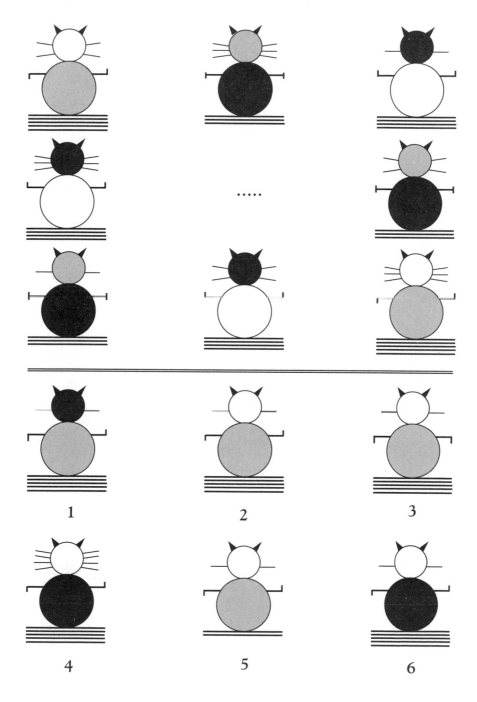

1

2

3

4

5

6

28) Which of the numbered figures best completes the series?

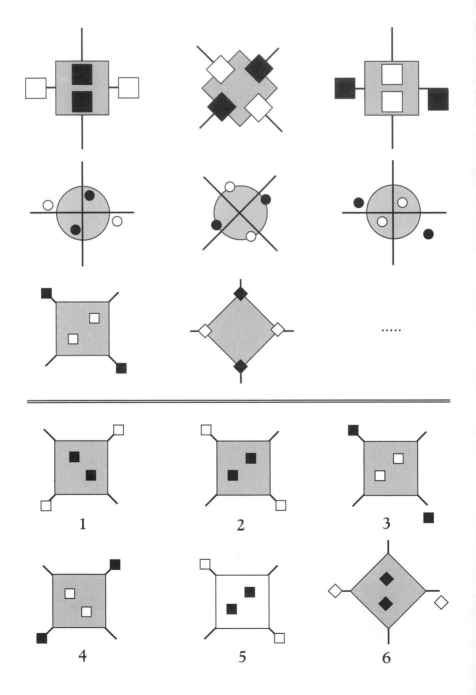

29) Which of these word anagrams is not an insect?

blyagdu

grauja

hrapsgpreso

etricck

thnoer

lfy

30) What word, added to each initial letter, forms new words?

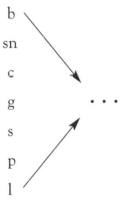

b

sn

c

g

s

p

l

. . .

31) What is the missing number?

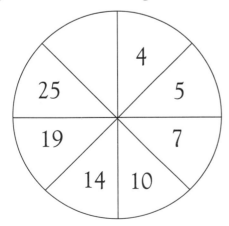

32) What number is missing from the final series?

6   5   8   7   4   8   9   3   .....

33) Complete the following analogy.

Japanese is to Asian as French is to .....

(a) American   (b) African   (c) European   (d) country

34) What are the missing numbers?

1   2   4   5   7   11   13

35) Which of the following figures does not belong?

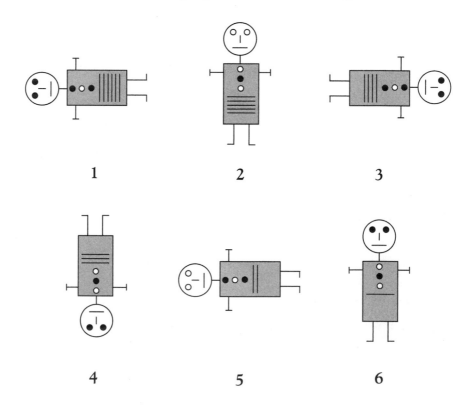

1   2   3

4   5   6

36) Which of the numbered figures best completes the series?

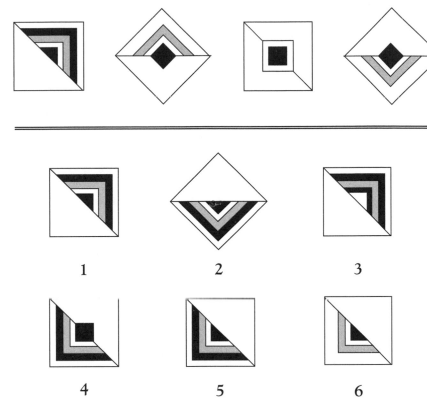

For test solutions, turn to page 68.

Test 4 Solutions

1) **2.** The two figures progressively approach one another.

2) **3.** The product of the three sets is 144.

3) **2.** The sum of the square and rhombus is 40.

4) **v.** The pattern progressively increases by +2, +3, +4, +5.

5) **hutch.** It's furniture, as opposed to: kitchen, corridor, bathroom, foyer.

6) **lace.**

7) concrete, pavement. Letters in words alternate.

8) **21.** Multiply the letters in the columns.

9) **4.**

10) **Krista.**

11) **30.** Multiply the numbers in the outside circles and subtract the number in the rhombus from the sum.

12) **c.**

13) **5.** The squares inside rotate clockwise.

14) **1.**

15) **4.** The sum of the bottom numbers is subtracted from the sum of the top numbers, and divided by 2.

16) **yellow.** It's the only warm color.

17) **1591.** Multiply the first two numbers then add +1 to the product.

18) **p.** The pattern alternatively skips letters +2, +1.

19) **343.**

20) **Siamese.** It's the only cat breed.

21) **c.** Ruble.

22) **9.** Divide the sum of the circles by 2.

23) **17.** It's the only number that is not divisible.

24) **ear.** The other words are: smell, hearing, sight, taste.

25) **16.** Multiply the first two numbers and then double the result.

26) **3.** It's the only figure with that is three-sided.

27) **2.** Each series, from lines and columns, has only one cat with: a white, gray, and black head and body; 1, 2, 3 whiskers; 5, 4, 3 baselines; and three different types of arm.

28) **2.** The figure rotates 45° clockwise. The white squares move outward while the black squares move inward.

29) **jaguar.** The other words are: ladybug, grasshopper, cricket, hornet, and fly.

30) **ore.**

31) **32.** The pattern is: +1, +2, +3, +4, +5, +6, +7.

32) **7.** The sum of the three sets is 19.

33) **c.**

34) **8, 10.** There are two patterns that increase by +3.

35) **5.** It's the only figure with the feet facing left.

36) **5.** The square is made up of four inner squares that decrease in one half section and increase in the other. The figure rotates 90°.

SELF-SCORING		
Less than 14 = Poor	–
From 15 to 19 = Adequate	☆
From 20 to 24 = Fair	☆
From 25 to 29 = Good	☆☆☆
From 30 to 36 = Excellent	☆☆☆☆

TEST 5

1) **Which of these word anagrams does not belong?**

   ofkr

   sptna

   fiken

   knanip

   sgsal

   opnso

2) **What are the missing numbers?**

   3   5   9   17   33   .....

   5   7   11   19   35   .....

3) **What letters, missing from the parentheses, complete these two common words?**

   ba (....) be

   su (....) ne

4) **What are the missing letters?**

c	g	n
f	j	q
i	m	t
.....	.....	.....

5) **Complete the following analogy.**

   451208 is to death as 20124519 is to .....

6) What numbers belong in the parentheses?

16 (26) 13

8 (...) 15

cad (12) aba

dai (...) fab

102 (6) 17

117 (...) 13

7) What are the missing numbers and letters?

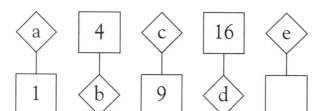

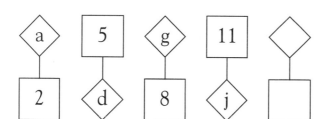

8) What number best completes the series?

4   2   7   13   .....

9) Which of the numbered figures best completes the series?

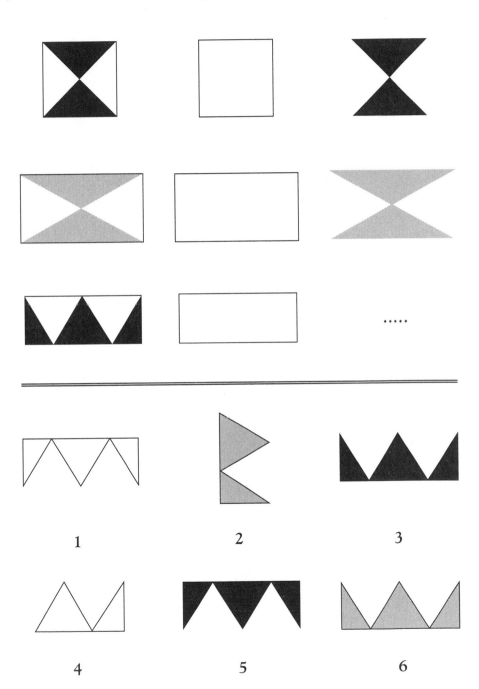

1

2

3

4

5

6

73

10) Choose the correct answer.

Victoria lives in a third-floor apartment under her cousin, Dawn. Veronica lives in the apartment above Sara, who lives under Victoria. Dawn, who lives on the very top floor, shares the staircase with Lisa, who lives in the apartment below Sara.

Who lives on the first floor?

(Victoria, Dawn, Veronica, Sara, Lisa)

On the third floor?

(Victoria, Dawn, Veronica, Sara, Lisa)

11) What number is missing from the triangle?

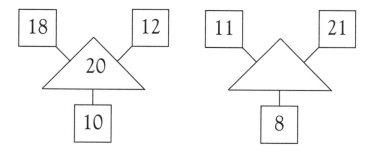

12) Choose the correct statement.

Blue is the prettiest color.

(a) Is always true.   (b) Is never true.
(c) Is sometimes true.   (d) Is an opinion

13) Which of the numbered figures best completes the series?

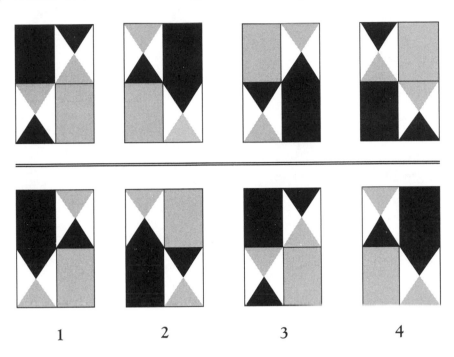

1   2   3   4

14) Complete the following analogy.

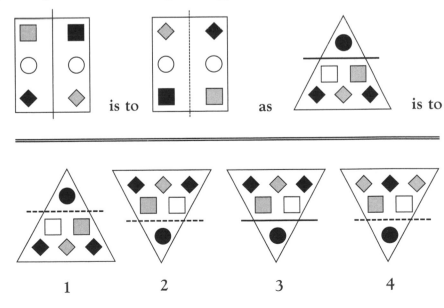

1   2   3   4

15) What number is missing from the circle?

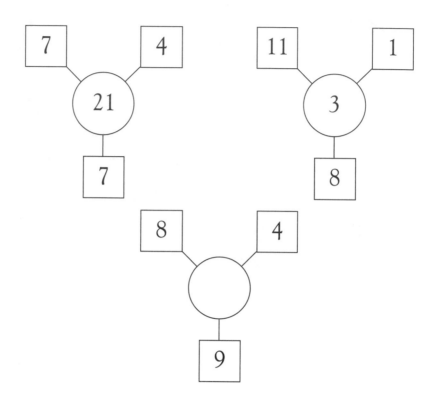

16) Which of these words does not belong?

Babylonians   Romans   Greeks
Phoenicians   Mayans

17) What are the missing numbers?

4   2   5   3   7   5   14   12

18) What letter best completes the series?

a   b   c   e   h   .....

19) **What number and letter are missing?**

    2   8   5   11   8   14   .....

    b   h   f   l   r   p   .....

20) **Which of these words does not belong?**

    mother   father   sister   aunt   niece

21) **Which of these words best completes the series?**

    well   boiling   mineral   natural   .....

    (a) shower   (b) faucet   (c) tower   (d) salt

22) **What numbers are missing from the squares?**

4	9	7
6		2
8	1	5

7	5	6
2		3
1	4	9

23) **Which two words are the most alike?**

    best   sillier   older   shortest   greater   worse

24) Which of these word anagrams does not belong?

genncaoi

ciganmsty

bclyeic

goirwn

lcgiycn

25) What is the missing number?

3   6   17

4   9   35

2   3   .....

26) Which of the these figures does not belong?

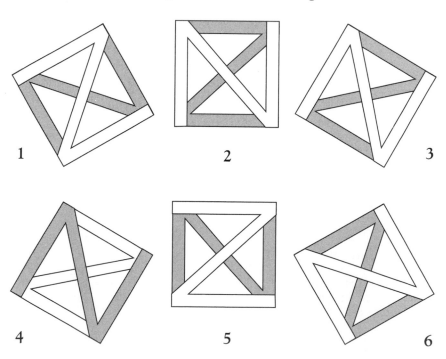

1   2   3

4   5   6

27) Which of the numbered figures best completes the series?

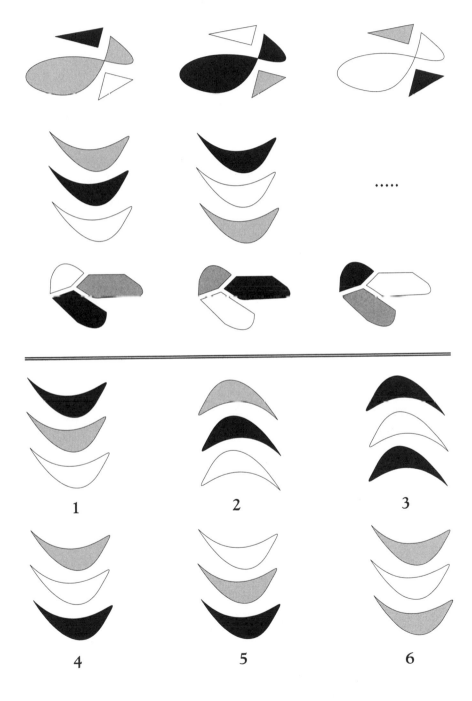

1

2

3

4

5

6

28) Which of the numbered figures best completes the series?

1

2

3

4

5

6

29) **Which of these word anagrams is not a tree?**

prujien

hrbci

cusrep

nettshcu

etentl

ilowwl

30) **What word, added to each initial letter, forms new words?**

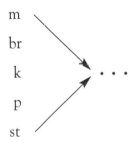

m

br

k

p

st

. . .

31) **What number is missing from the chart?**

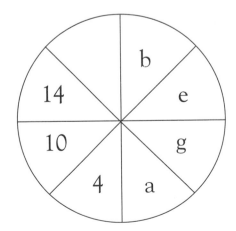

32) What number best completes the series?

　　5　9　17　33　.....

33) Complete the following analogy.

　　Red is to blood as blue is to .....

　　(a) orange　(b) blue　(c) sky　(d) air

34) What number best completes the series?

　　8　13　22　37　62　.....

35) Which of the following figures does not belong?

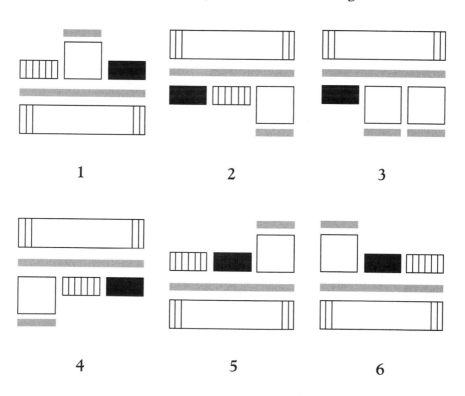

　　　1　　　　　　　　2　　　　　　　　3

　　　4　　　　　　　　5　　　　　　　　6

36) Which of the numbered figures best completes the series?

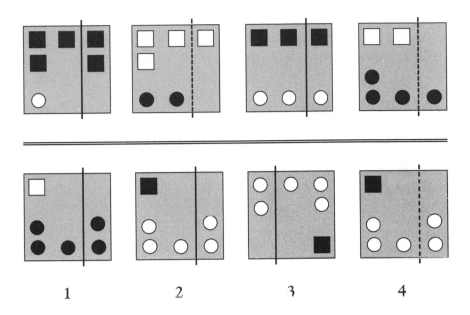

1   2   3   4

For test solutions, turn to page 84.

Test 5 Solutions

1) **pants.** The others are: fork, knife, napkin, glass, and spoon.

2) **65, 67.** The pattern increases by +2, +4, +16, +32.

3) **thro, nshi.**

4) **l, p, w.** The pattern vertically skips two letters.

5) **taxes.** Numerical order of letters.

6) **15.** Multiply the numbers outside the parentheses and divide the result by 8.
23. Add the letters together.
9. Divide the first number by the second number.

7) **25.** Square the number of the letter. **m, 14.** Diagonally skip two numbers and two letters.

8) **90.** Multiply the first number with the second number, the second with the third. etc., and add 1 to their products.

9) **3.** Subtract the first figure from the second figure.

10) **Lisa. Victoria and Veronica.**

11) **20.** Add the numbers in the squares and divide the sum by 2.

12) **d.**

13) **3.** Every rectangle in the figure moves clockwise.

14) **2.** The figure turns 190° horizontally, changing the positions of the shaded elements. The line changes from solid to dotted.

15) **23.** Multiply the numbers in the top squares and subtract the result from the bottom square.

16) **Mayans.** It's the only Western Hemisphere civilization.

17) **10, 8.** There are two alternate patterns that increase by 3.

18) **m.** The sum of the first and second letters equals the third letter. The sum of the second and third letters equals the fourth letter, etc.

19) **11.** There are two alternate patterns that increase by 3.
n. There are alternate patterns that skip 3 letters.

20) **father.** It's the only masculine reference.

21) **d.**

22) **3, 8.** Each square contains one decimal number, from 1 to 9.

23) **best, shortest.** They are superlatives, not comparatives.

24) **Bicycle.** The other words are activities: canoeing, gymnastics, racing, rowing, cycling.

25) **5.** Multiply the first two numbers, subtract 1 from the product.

26) **4.** The white Z is always in the first dimension.

27) **5.** The pattern alternates among white, gray, and black.

28) **4.** Each column has: a black, gray, and white roof; 1, 2, and 3 base lines; and black, gray, and white windows.

29) **nettle.** It's a shrub, not a tree. The others are juniper, birch, spruce, chestnut, and willow.

30) **ink.**

31) **2.** Multiply the letters by 2.

32) **65.** Double every number and subtract 1.

33) **c.**

34) **103.** Add the first and the second number, the second and the third number, and so on, and progressively add +1, +2, +3, +4 to the sums.

35) **3.** The other figures have: one black rectangle, one lined rectangle, and one white square.

36) **2.** One square is subtracted and one circle is added. Both squares and circles alternate from black to white. The dividing line alternates from solid to dotted.

SELF-SCORING

Less than 14	=	Poor	–
From 15 to 19	=	Adequate	☆
From 20 to 24	=	Fair	☆
From 25 to 29	=	Good	☆☆☆
From 30 to 36	=	Excellent	☆☆☆☆

TEST 6

1) **Which of these word anagrams does not belong?**

   gboin

   noplomyo

   shces

   prkeo

   sipbho

   nosmiode

2) **What number is missing from the final square?**

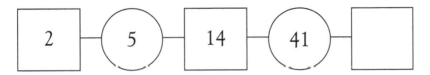

3) **What letters, added to the parentheses, complete one word and start the second?**

   gu (...) oge

   bl (...) ay

4) **What is the missing letter?**

c	e	h
a	f	g
c	b	e
d	h	.....

5) **Complete the following analogy.**

   Armadillo is to 245263889 as radio is to .....

6) What number is missing from the circle?

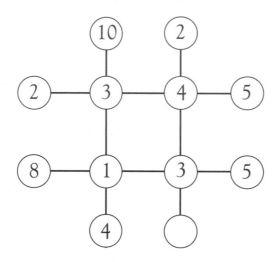

7) What numbers are missing from the squares?

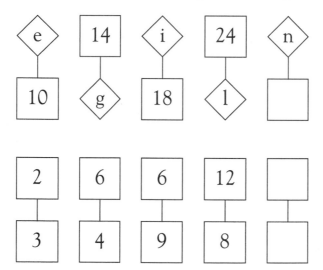

8) What number best completes this series?

8   6   12   16   26   .....

9) Which of the numbered figures best completes the series?

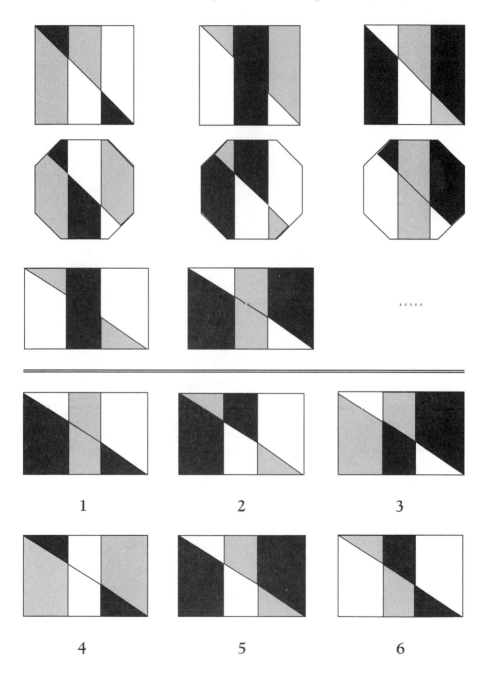

1

2

3

4

5

6

10) What number is missing from the chart?

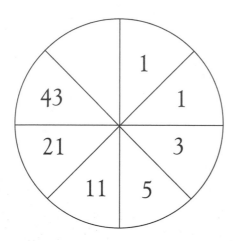

11) What number is missing from the triangle?

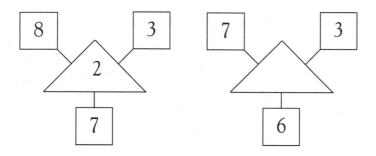

12) Choose the correct statement.

Dogs are purebred.

(a) Is always true   (b) Is never true
(c) Is sometimes true   (d) Is an opinion

13) Which of the numbered figures best completes the series?

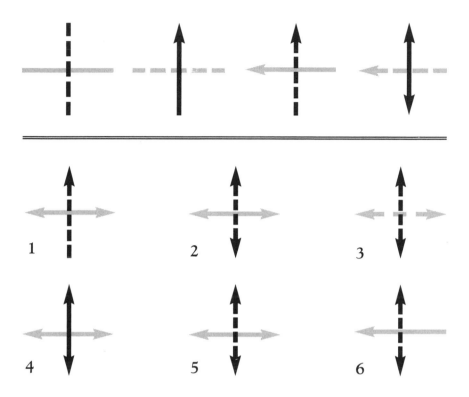

14) Complete the following analogy.

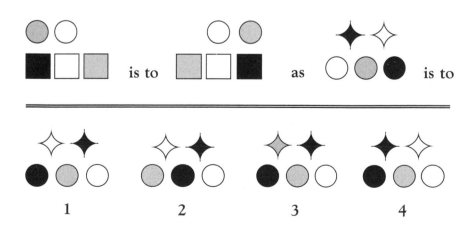

15) What number is missing from the circle?

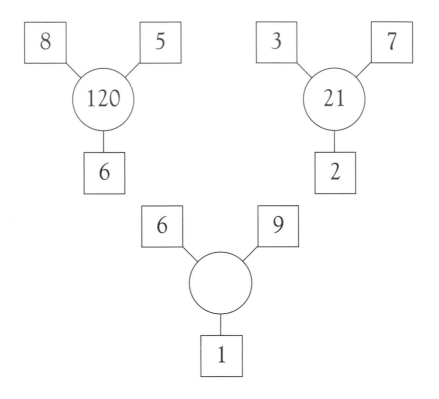

16) Which of these words does not belong?

train   brain   table   sable   fairy
gnome   carton   wagon

17) What are the missing numbers?

3   6   8   16   21   104   154

18) What letter best completes the series?

b   d   g   j   .....

19) **What are the missing letters?**

20) **Complete the following analogy.**

6 is to 36 as 8 is to .....

21) **Which of these words best completes the series?**

seaquake   earthquake   flood   avalanche   .....

(a) sea   (b) catastrophe   (c) tornado   (d) fire

22) **What numbers are missing from the squares?**

3	8	5
4	3	4
6		4

7	1	4
2	7	3
4		6

23) **Which of these words does not belong?**

seventeen   thirteen   eleven

eighteen   seventy-three   seven

24) **Which of these word anagrams does not belong?**

rervid

actapni

rsalio

wabaitson

dalmair

25) **What is the missing number?**

6	7	21
8	9	36
10	4	.....

26) **Which of the following figures does not belong?**

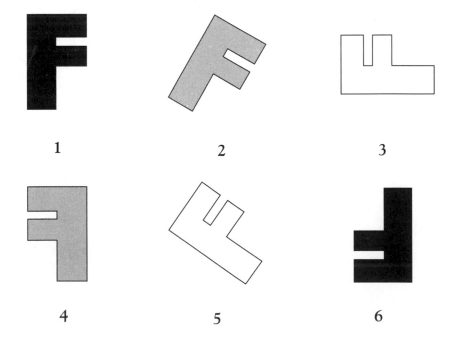

27) Which of the numbered figures best completes the series?

1

2

3

4

5

6

28) Which of the numbered figures best completes the series?

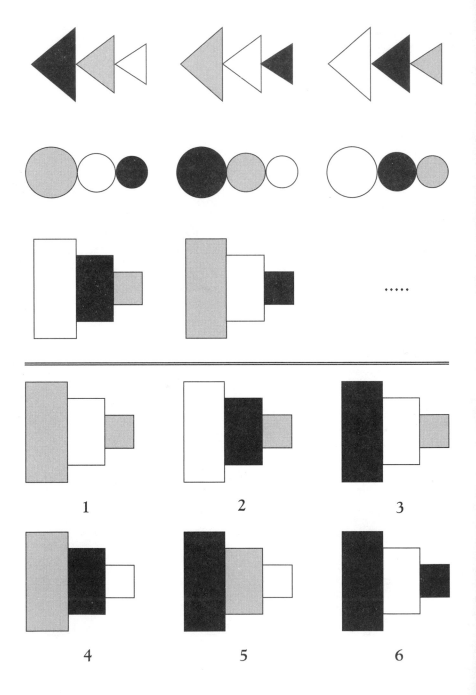

29) **Which of these word anagrams does not belong?**

    hogloscypy

    stmachimeta

    anlit

    michtesry

    syhcsip

    loshoc

30) **What word, added to each initial letter, forms new words?**

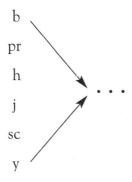

31) **What are the missing letters?**

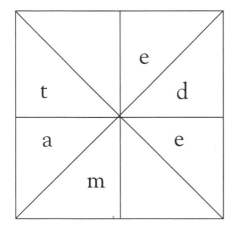

32) What number best completes the series?

1   2   6   16   .....

33) Complete the following analogy.

Shakespeare is to poetry as Verdi is to .....

(a) music   (b) opera   (c) art   (d) note

34) What number best completes the series?

3   2   4   4   8   16   .....

35) Which of the following figures does not belong?

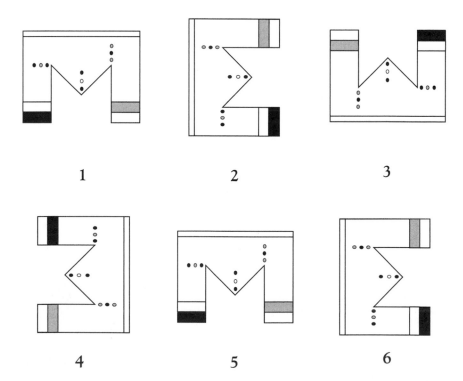

1   2   3

4   5   6

36) Which of the numbered figures best completes the series?

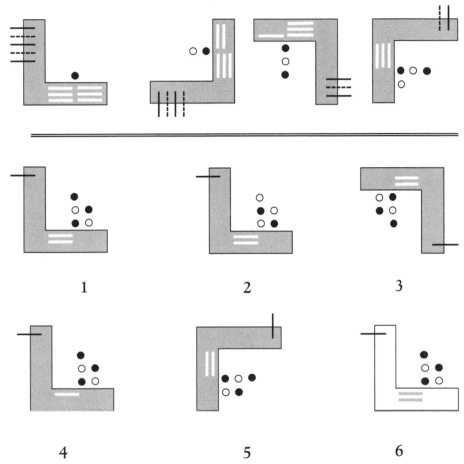

1   2   3

4   5   6

For test solutions, turn to page 100.

Test 6 Solutions

1) **bishop.** The other words are: bingo, Monopoly, chess, poker, dominoes.

2) **122.** Multiply by 3 and subtract 1 from the product.

3) **sto, ess.**

4) **l.** Add the numeric values of the first two letters.

5) **42639.** Numerical order of letters.

6) **5.** The product of each line is 120.

7) **28.** The numeric value of the letter is doubled.
10, 15. Starting at the top, add +2 to every number diagonally. Starting at the bottom, add +3 to every number diagonally.

8) **40.** Progressively add two numbers and subtract 2 from the sum.

9) **4.** The colors rotate clockwise while alternating among white, black, and gray.

10) **85.** Starting with 1, multiply every number by 2 and alternately adjust the product by −1, +1.

11) **2.** Add the numbers in the top squares and subtract the number in the bottom square from the sum. Then divide by 2.

12) **c.**

13) **2.** The arrow progressively builds while alternating between the solid and dotted lines. Both lines also alternate between 1st and 2nd dimensions.

14) **1.** The figure is a mirror image of itself.

15) **27.** Multiply all the numbers in the squares and divide the product by 2.

16) **carton.** It's the only word with six letters.

17) **41, 57.** Add the first and the second numbers, the second and the third numbers, and so on, while progressively adjusting the sums by −1, +2, −3, +4, −5, +6, −7.

18) **l.** The series is every second consonant. Add the numeric values of the numbers.

19) **u, u, m.** The formed word is "autumn."

20) **64.** It is the square of the numbers.

21) **c.** The phenomina progressively gain altitude.

22) **4, 5.** All three vertical columns in each box have the same sum.

23) **eighteen.** The other numbers are all prime.

24) **driver.** The other words are: captain, sailor, boatswain, admiral.

25) **20.** Multiply the first two numbers and divide the product by 2.

26) **4.** The figure continually rotates but does not overturn.

27) **4.** Each house has 1 black, white, and gray roof; 1, 2, and 3 base lines.

28) **5.** The pattern alternates among black, white, and gray figures.

29) **school.** The other words are class subjects: psychology, mathematics, Latin, chemistry, physics.

30) **owl.**

31) **s, p.** Stampede, reading counterclockwise.

32) **44.** Add two consecutive numbers, and multiply the sum by 2.

33) **b.**

34) **96.** Multiply the first and the second numbers, the second and the third numbers, and so on, progressively adjusting the products by −2, −4, −8, −16, −32.

35) **4.** The first rectangle on the left is always white.

36) **1.** The black lines progressively decrease and the white lines rotate 90° clockwise.

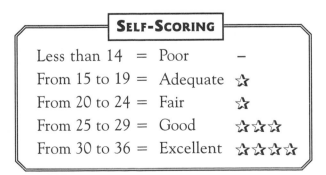

SELF-SCORING		
Less than 14 = Poor	–	
From 15 to 19 = Adequate	☆	
From 20 to 24 = Fair	☆	
From 25 to 29 = Good	☆☆☆	
From 30 to 36 = Excellent	☆☆☆☆	

TEST 7

1) Which of the numbered figures best completes the series?

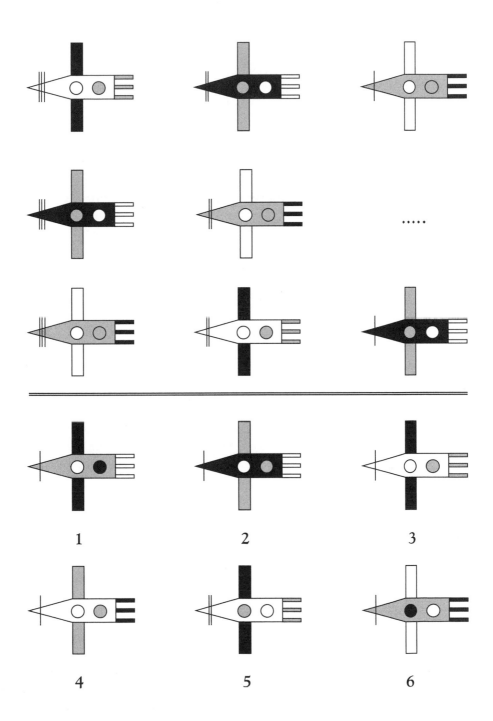

1

2

3

4

5

6

2) What number is missing from the square?

5	15	10
25	6	5
2	15	...

3) What number is missing from the base of the figure?

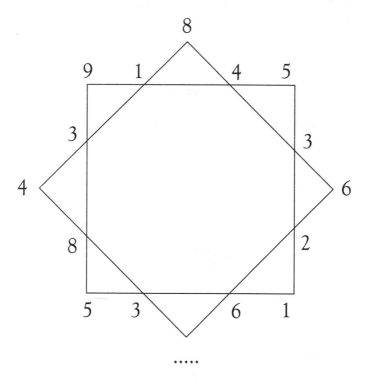

4) What is the missing letter?

v   t   q   m   .....

5) **Which of these word anagrams does not belong?**

    narfec

    niemtva

    sirsau

    asakal

    oguaplrt

6) **What is the missing word?**

    forage (road) paddock

    paltry (....) enemy

7) **What letters, added to the parentheses, complete one word and start the second?**

    to (...) ral

8) **What number is missing from the square?**

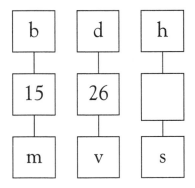

9) **Complete the following analogy.**

    12 is to 144 as 11 is to .....

10) Choose the correct answer.

Erica took the train to Detroit before Molly, but not before Emma. Martha took the train before Erica, but not before Emma.

Who took the last train?

(Erica, Molly, Emma, Martha)

11) What number is missing from the square?

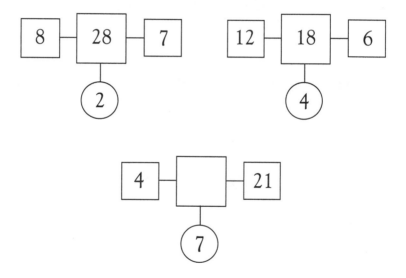

12) Choose the correct statement.

All rivers flow into the sea.

(a) Is always true   (b) Is never true

(c) Is sometimes true   (d) Is an opinion

13) Which of the numbered figures best completes the series.

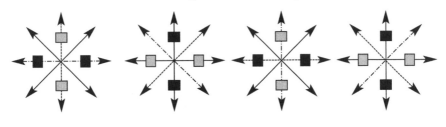

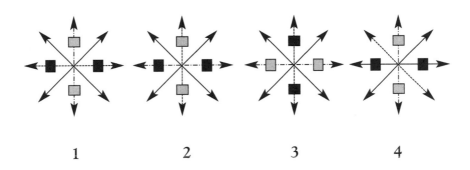

| 1 | 2 | 3 | 4 |

14) Complete the following analogy.

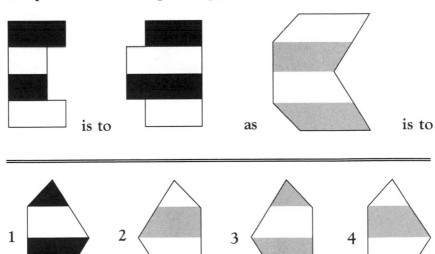

107

15) What number is missing from the square?

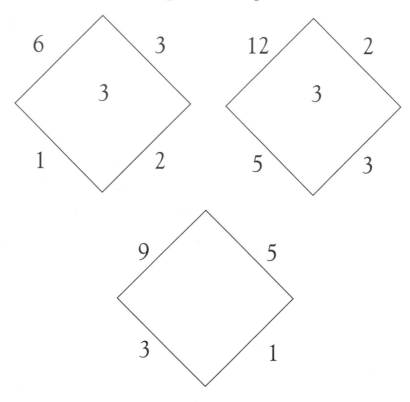

16) Which of these items does not belong?

bikini   t-shirt   sandals   overcoat   clogs   shorts

17) What number best completes the series?

4   3   11   32   351   .....

18) What letter best completes the series?

c   d   f   i   m   .....

19) Complete the following analogy.

512 is to 8 as 1331 is to .....

20) Which of these words does not belong?

Abyssinian   Chihuahua   Persian

Siamese   Carthusian   Burmese

21) Choose the answer that best completes the series.

Aphrodite   Apollo   Artemis   Athena   .....

(a) Aurora   (b) Poseidon   (c) Thor   (d) Venus

22) What number is missing from the square?

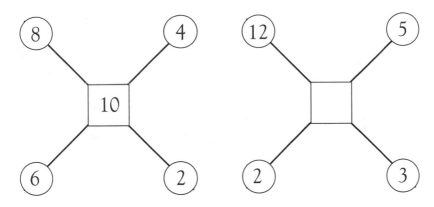

23) Which of the following numbers does not belong?

411   899   17   1365   7

2649   93   358   25   51

24) Which of these word anagrams does not belong?

snomono

ruanchier

roodnta

groduth

notpyoh

25) What is the missing number?

2   4   24

7   4   84

5   3   .....

26) Which of the following figures does not belong?

1

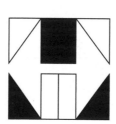

2

3

4

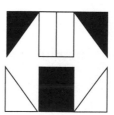

5

6

27) Which of the numbered figures best completes the series?

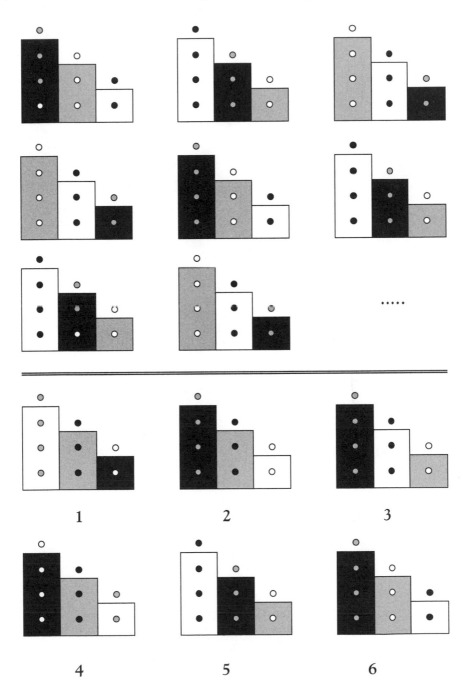

1

2

3

4

5

6

28) Which of the numbered figures best completes the series?

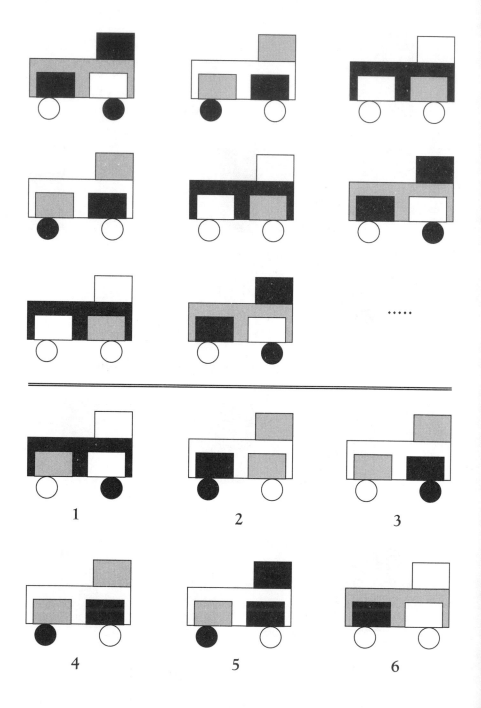

29) **Which of these word anagrams does not belong?**

    inono

    sicaphn

    opatto

    catripo

    gabaceb

    rocrta

30) **What word, added to each initial letter, forms new words?**

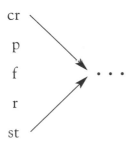

31) **What two letters are missing from the chart?**

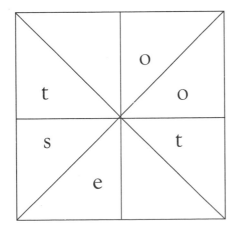

32) What number best completes the final series?

7   6   9   8   5   9   10   4   .....

33) Complete the following analogy.

Robinson is to baseball as Ashe is to .....

(a) billiards   (b) bowling   (c) tennis   (d) soccer

34) What numbers complete the series?

2   3   6   9   10   21   18

35) Which of the following figures does not belong?

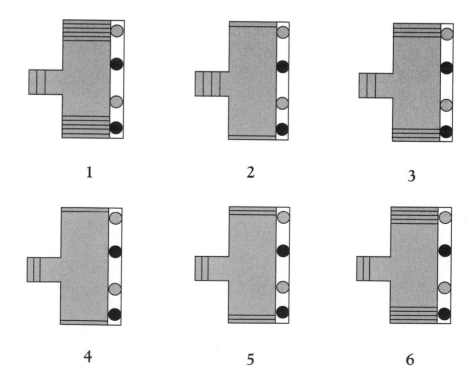

1   2   3

4   5   6

36) Which figure best completes the series?

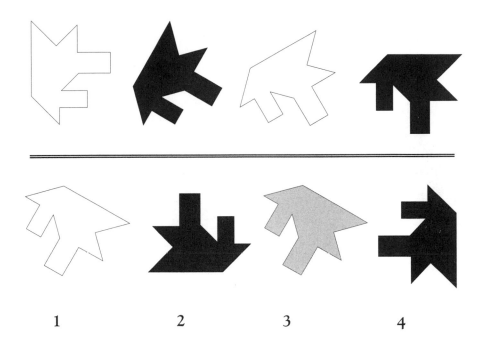

1   2   3   4

For test solutions, turn to page 116.

Test 7 Solutions

1) **3.** Each component of the figure alternates shading.

2) **25.** The product of each horizontal column is 750.

3) **2.** The sum is 50.

4) **h.** The pattern progressively decreases by –2, –3, –4, and –5.

5) **Alaska.** The others are countries: France, Vietnam, Russia, and Portugal.

6) **lane.**

7) **ast.**

8) **27.** Add up the numeric values of the letters.

9) **121.** The number squared.

10) **Molly.**

11) **12.** Multiply the numbers in the outside squares and divide the product by the number in the circle.

12) **b.**

13) **2.** The figure rotates 45°. The rectangles alternate between black and gray.

14) **2.**

15) **5.** Subtract the sums of the top and bottom numbers and divide the sum by 2.

16) **overcoat.** It's the only article of winter wear.

17) **11231.** Multiply the first number with the second number, the second with the third, etc., and subtract 1 from their products.

18) **r.** Progressively go through the alphabet, adding +1, +2, +3, +4, etc.

19) **11.** It is the cube's radical.

20) **Chihuahua.** It's the only dog breed.

21) **Poseidon.** They are all Greek gods.

22) **11.** Add the outside circles and divide the sum by 2.

23) **358.** It is the only even number.

24) **drought.** The other choices are storm conditions: monsoon, hurricane, tornado, typhoon.

25) **45.** Multiply the first two numbers and the product by 3.

26) **4.** Every figure has four black and white spaces.

27) **4.** The series alternates among black, white, and gray with the different components of the figures.

28) **5.** The pattern alternates among black, gray, and white within the figures.

29) **apricot.** It's the only fruit. The other words are vegetables: onion, spinach, potato, cabbage, and carrot.

30) **eel.**

31) **f, r.** Footrest.

32) **8.** The sum of each set is 22.

33) **c.** Tennis.

34) **15, 14.** The first pattern increases by +4, the second pattern increases by +6.

35) **2.** There are two lines on the left extension of the figure.

36) **1.** The figure rotates 30° and alternates between white and gray.

SELF-SCORING

Less than 14	= Poor	–
From 15 to 19	= Adequate	☆
From 20 to 24	= Fair	☆
From 25 to 29	= Good	☆☆☆
From 30 to 36	= Excellent	☆☆☆☆

SPECIFIC TESTS

NUMERICAL

TEST

1) What is the missing number?

  13   18   15   20   17   22   .....

2) What number is missing from the final square?

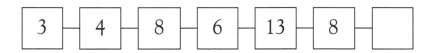

3) What numbers are missing from the squares?

7	3	7
5	8	4
6	2	

7	9	4
5	6	9
5		5

4) What is the missing number?

  5   4   10
  8   4   16
  6   3   .....

5) What is the missing number?

  4   3   14   34   96   .....

6) What number is missing from the circle?

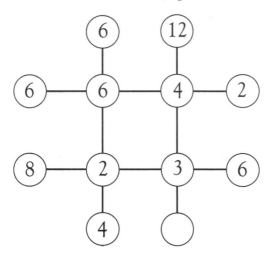

7) What numbers are missing from the squares?

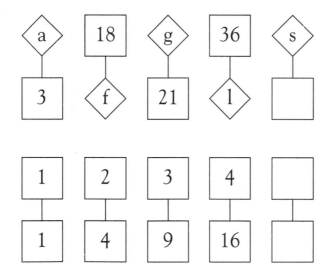

8) What is the missing number?

4   2   3   2   2   .....

9) **What are the missing numbers?**

    5   1   5   7   11   49

10) **What number is missing from this chart?**

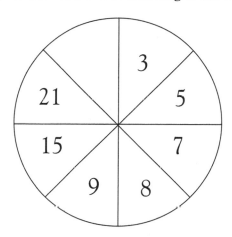

11) **What number is missing from the triangle?**

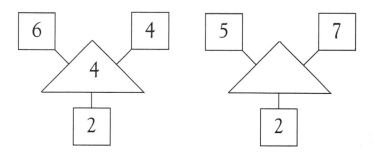

12) **Complete the following analogies.**

    216 is to 108 as 96 is to .....

    27 is to 9 as 36 is to .....

13) What is the missing number?

2	2	8
1	2	4
3	2	.....

14) What number is missing from the square?

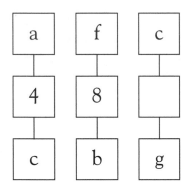

15) What numbers are missing from the parentheses?

13 (11) 16
15 (....) 18

fab (18) dad
cai (....) baa

126 (7) 18
288 (....) 32

16) **What number is missing from the circle?**

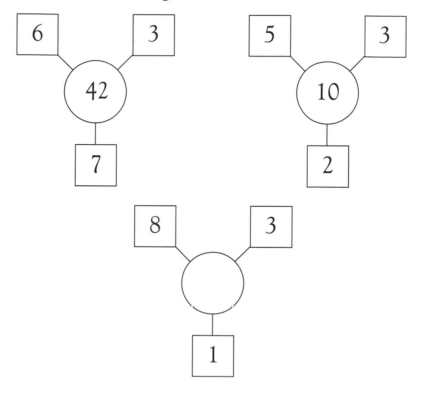

17) **Complete the following analogies.**

5 is to 10 as 6 is to .....

2 is to 8 as 5 is to .....

18) **What numbers best complete the series?**

3   1   4   2   6   4   13   11   18

19) **What number best completes the series?**

     1   2   5   26   .....

20) **What number is missing from the center square?**

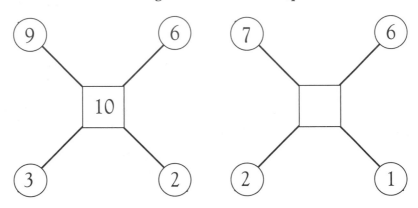

21) **What number is missing from the final series?**

     3   1   7   2   1   8   5   3   .....

22) **What numbers are missing from the squares?**

17	11	3
18	6	6
10	2	

13	5	4
15	9	3
5	1	

23) What number is missing from the square?

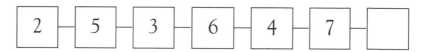

24) Which number does not belong?

2   8   15   16   18

264   86   322   14

25) What is the missing number?

4   2   6

8   5   9

9   3   18

7   2   .....

26) What number is missing from the square?

6	2	3

3	4	3

9	2	

125

27) What number is missing from the square?

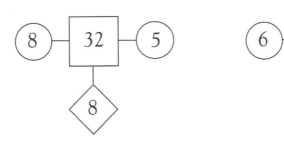

28) What number best completes the series?

4   7   15   29   59   .....

29) What is the missing number?

1   3   6   6
9   2   2   12
5   3   4   .....

30) What number best completes the series?

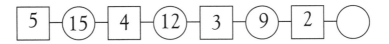

31) What number best completes the series?

5   4   10   20   100   .....

32) **What number is missing from the base of the figure?**

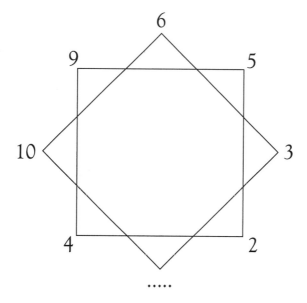

For test solutions, turn to page 128.

Numerical Test Solutions

1) **19.** The pattern alternates between +5 and –3.

2) **18.** Two patterns alternate, +5 and +2.

3) **9, 10.** Totalled horizontally, the sum of the numbers in the columns are 17 and 20 respectively.

4) **9.** Multiply the numbers in the first two columms and divide the product by two.

5) **260.** Add the first number to the second number, the second to the third, etc., multiplying the sum by two.

6) **2.** The product of every line, both horizontally and vertically, is 288.

7) **57.** The numeric value of each letter is multiplied by 3.
   5, 25. The top number is squared.

8) **1.** Add the first number with the second number, the second with the third, etc., and subtract 3 from the sums.

9) **19, 29.** Add the first number to the second number, the second with the third, etc., alternately subtracting –1, +1 to the sums.

10) **24.** Multiply the opposite numbers by 3.

11) **5.** Add the numbers in the top squares and subtract the sum from the number in the bottom square and divide it by 2.

12) **48, 12.**

13) **12.** Multiply the first two numbers and then multiply the product by 2.

14) **10.** Add the numeric values of the letters vertically.

15) **15.** Add each number outside the parentheses.
    17. Add the value of each letter outside the parentheses.
    9. Divide the number before the parentheses by the number after.

16) **8.** Multiply the numbers in the squares and divide the product by 3.

17) **12, 125.** Doubled and squared.

18) **9, 7.** Two patterns increase by +1, +2, +3, +4, etc.

19) **677.** Multipy each number by itself and add +1.

20) **10.** Add the numbers in the top circles and subtract it from the sum of the bottom circles.

21) **3.** The sum of all three sets is 11.

22) **4, 2.** Subtract the numbers in the first two columns and divide by 2.

23) **5.** The pattern progressively increases/decreases by +3 and –2.

24) **15.** It is the only odd number.

25) **15.** Subtract the first two numbers and multiply the sum by 3.

26) **2.** The product of each horizontal column is 36.

27) **30.** Multiply the numbers in the circles and subtract the product by the number in the rhombus.

28) **117.** Double the number and alternately subtract/add –1 and +1.

29) **20.** Multiply the first three numbers and divide the product by 3.

30) **6.** Multiply the numbers in the squares by 3.

31) **1000.** Multiply the first number by the second number, the second by the third, etc., and divide the products by 2.

32) **2.** The products of the rhombus and square 360.

SELF-SCORING

Less than 14 =	Poor	–
From 15 to 18 =	Adequate	☆
From 19 to 22 =	Fair	☆
From 23 to 26 =	Good	☆☆☆
From 27 to 32 =	Excellent	☆☆☆☆

VERBAL TEST

1) Which of these word anagrams does not belong?

sheor

greit

inol

prentha

heplante

chroserino

2) What word, added to the initial letters, forms other words?

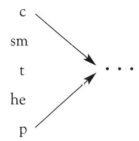

3) What is the missing word?

music (suit) miter

lapel (....) aster

4) Which of these word anagrams does not belong?

uplot

truepji

runats

usn

cyrruem

sevnu

5) Complete the following analogy.

Missouri is to river as Huron is to ....

(a) sea   (b) island   (c) lake   (d) promontory

6) Choose the correct answer.

Paul reached the top of the mountain before Mark, but not before Luke. Morgan reached the top after his brother Robert, but before Luke.

Who reached the top last?

(Paul, Mark, Luke, Morgan, Robert)

7) What word, added to the initial letters, forms other words?

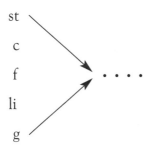

st

c

f   . . . .

li

g

8) Choose the correct statement.

All roads lead to Rome.

(a) Is always true (b) Is never true
(c) Is sometimes true (d) Is an opinion

9) Choose the correct word.

auto   beau   adieu   ouzo   ....

(a) epee   (b) tabu   (c) cocoa   (d) rout

10) Which of these word anagrams does not belong?

netsin

csocer

obellllavy

elbatblkas

gicbylinc

blwogin

11) Which of these words does not belong?

square   circle   rectangle
octagon   pyramid   triangle

12) What is the missing word?

radish (date) steam

brain   (...)   riddle

13) Choose the answer next in series.

Aries   Taurus   Gemini   Cancer   Leo   .....

(a) Virgo (b) Capricorn (c) Aquarius (d) Pisces

14) Which of these word anagrams does not belong?

chrib

kao

cutsethn

yiv

nipe

133

15) What is the missing word?

prune (unit) sting

slate (....) smoke

16) What word, added to the initial letters, forms other words?

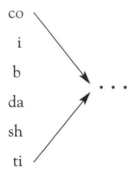

co

i

b

da

sh

ti

17) Which of these word anagrams does not belong?

gero

rafiy

mogen

scroerses

fael

lfe

18) Choose the correct answer.

Lucy finished the puzzle before Beth, but not before Betty. Hannah finished after Hazel but before her sister, Betty.

Who finished the puzzle first?

(Lucy, Beth, Betty, Hannah, Hazel)

19) **Which of these words does not belong?**

rain   fog   lightning   snow   cloud   hail

20) **What word, added to the initial letters, forms other words?**

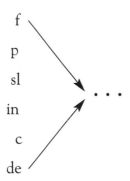

21) **Choose the correct statement.**

No fish is a mammal.

(a) Is always true   (b) Is never true

(c) Is sometimes true   (d) Is an opinion

22) **Choose the correct answer.**

Morris finished his quiz twenty minutes before Philip, but not before Larry. Carlos finished his quiz after his brother Manuel, but before Morris.

Who finished the quiz last?

(Morris, Philip, Larry, Manuel, Carlos)

23) **Complete the following analogy.**

White is to mountain as Yellow is to .....

(a) ocean   (b) island   (c) river   (d) stream

24) Choose the correct answer.

While riding horses, Manuel rode faster than Patrick, but not as fast as Lawrence. Martin rode faster than his brother, Thomas, who rode faster than Lawrence.

Who was the slowest?

(Manuel, Patrick, Martin, Lawrence, Thomas)

25) What word, added to the initial letters, forms other words?

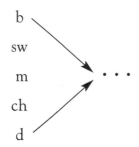

b
sw
m
ch
d

. . .

26) Which of these words does not belong?

towel   echo   book   dresser
window   hoof   computer

27) Complete the following analogy.

Library is to book as book is to .....

(a) binding   (b) copy   (c) page   (d) cover

28) What is the missing word?

camel (time) quite

pasta (....) elope

29) Which of these word anagrams does not belong?

meoro

lichame

kmra

tyhonan

ilas

lapu

30) What letters, added to the parentheses, complete one word and start the second?

ti (...) bil

om (...) iny

fl (...) hs

31) What is the missing word?

wrong (goal) alert

sushi   (....)   legal

32) Choose the correct answer.

Simon left the house the house a half hour before Alex, but one hour after Bert. Ryan left the house fifteen minutes before his brother, Roger, who left five minutes after Bert.

Who left first?

(Simon, Alex, Bert, Ryan, Roger)

For solutions, turn to page 138.

Verbal Test Solutions

1) **horse.** It's the only domestic animal. The other animals are: tiger, lion, panther, elephant, and rhinoceros.

2) **art.**

3) **past.**

4) **sun.** It's a star, not a planet. The other words are: Pluto, Jupiter, Saturn, Mercury, and Venus.

5) **c.**

6) **Mark.**

7) **able.**

8) **b.**

9) **epee.** All the words are made up of a series of vowels with only one consonent.

10) **bicycling.** It's the only sport that does not use a ball. The other words are: tennis, soccer, volleyball, basketball, and bowling.

11) **pyramid.** It's the only solid figure.

12) **arid.**

13) **a.**

14) **ivy.** It is not a tree; the others are: birch, oak, chestnut, and pine.

15) **atom.**

16) **red.**

17) **flea.** It is an insect. The other choices are mythical characters: ogre, fairy, gnome, sorceress, and elf.

18) **Hazel.**

19) **lightning.** The only weather word that does not contain moisture.

20) **lay.**

21) **a.**

22) **Philip.**

23) **c.**

24) **Patrick.**

25) **ill.**

26) **echo.** It is not tangiblecannot be touched.

27) **c.**

28) **post.**

29) **Lisa.** It's the only female name. The others are: Romeo, Michael, Mark, Anthony, and Paul.

30) **ger, bra, oat.**

31) **isle.**

32) **Ryan.**

SELF-SCORING		
Less than 14	= Poor	—
From 15 to 18	= Adequate	☆
From 19 to 22	= Fair	☆
From 23 to 26	= Good	☆☆☆
From 27 to 32	= Excellent	☆☆☆☆

SPATIAL
TEST

1) Which of the numbered figures best completes the series?

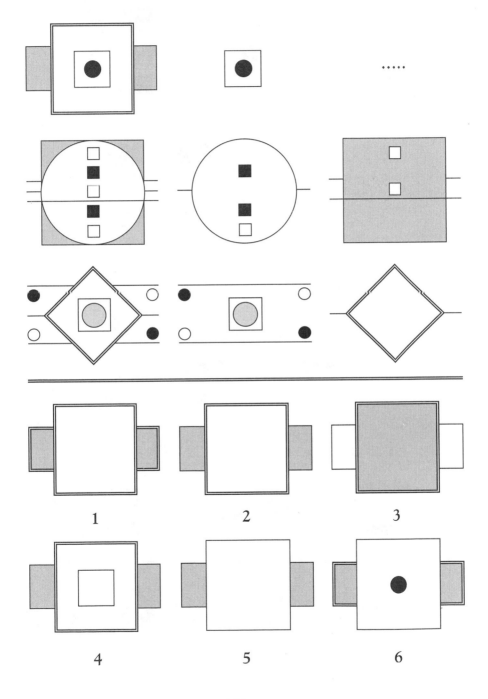

2) Which numbered figure is next in the series?

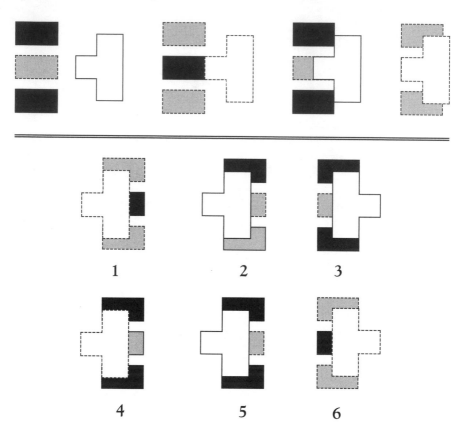

3) Complete the following analogy.

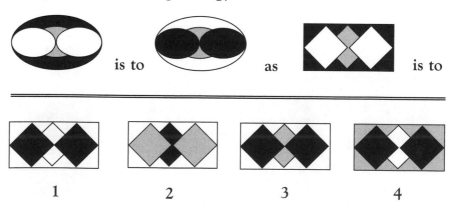

4) Which numbered figure is next in the series?

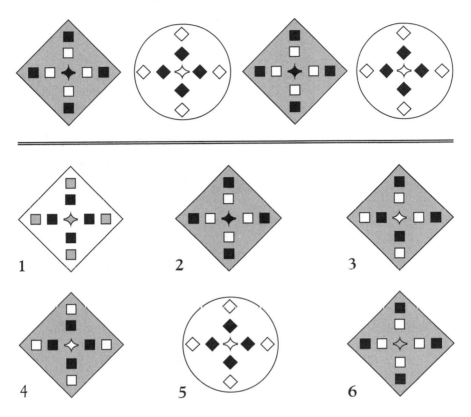

5) Which of the following figures does not belong?

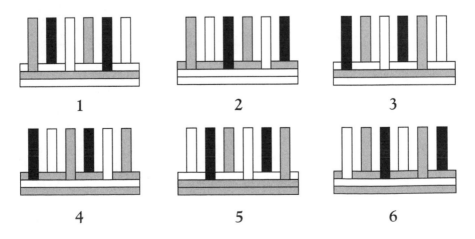

6) Which of the following figures does not belong?

1   2   3

4   5   6

7) Which of the following figures does not belong?

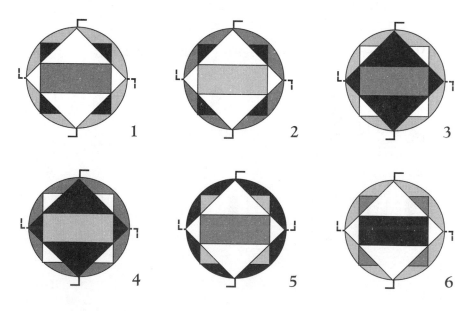

1   2   3

4   5   6

8) Which of the numbered figures is next in the series?

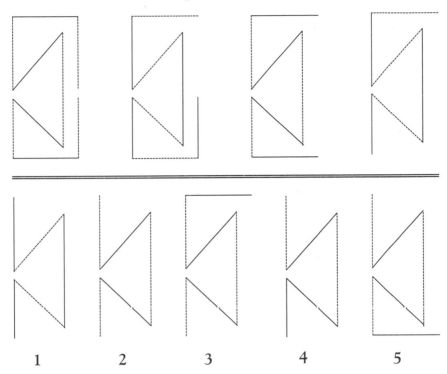

9) Complete the following analogy.

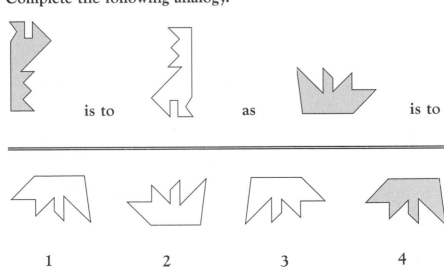

145

10) Which of the numbered figures best completes the series?

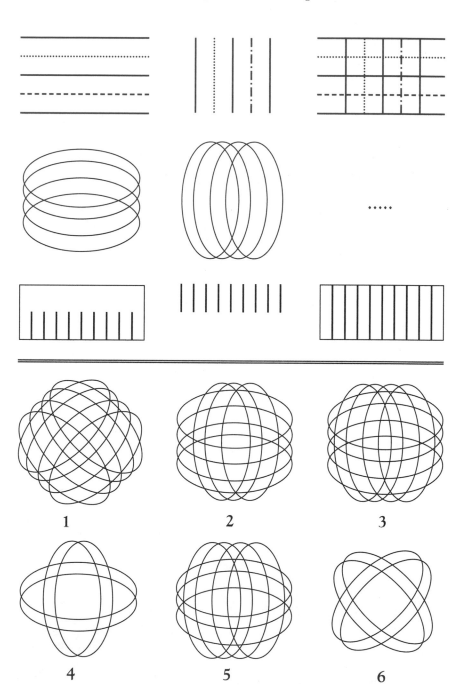

11) Which of the numbered figures is next in the series?

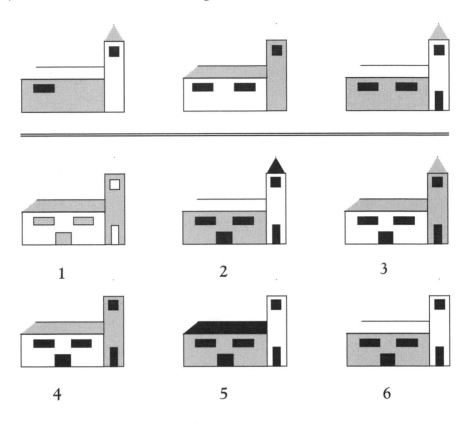

12) Which of the following figures does not belong?

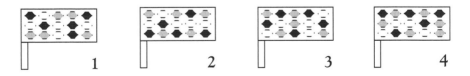

13) Which of the following figures does not belong?

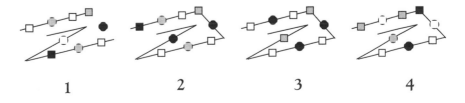

14) Which of the following figures does not belong?

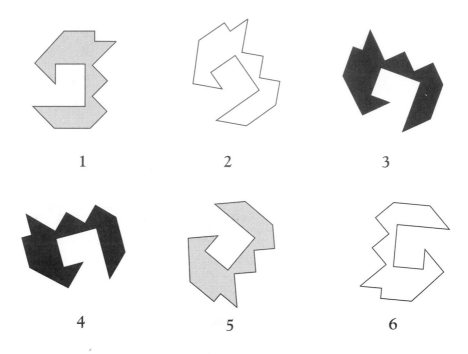

1   2   3

4   5   6

15) Which of the following figures does not belong?

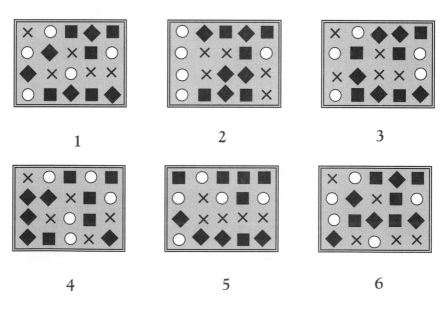

1   2   3

4   5   6

16) Which of the numbered figures is next in the series?

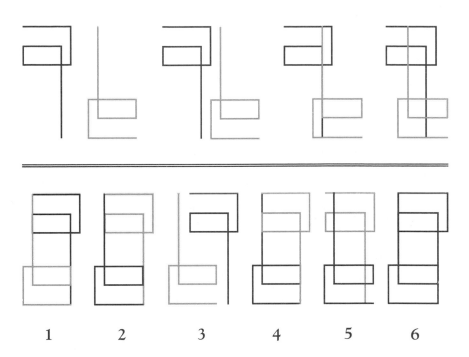

1   2   3   4   5   6

17) Complete the following analogy.

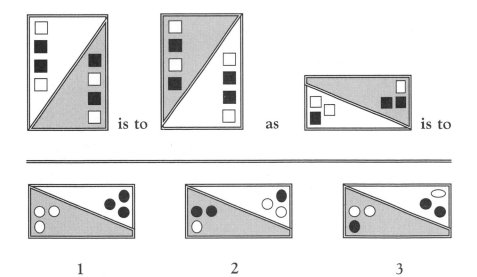

1   2   3

18) Which of the numbered figures comes next in the series?

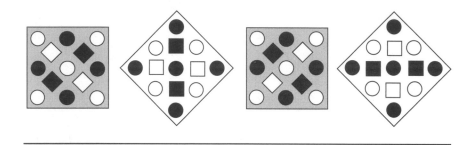

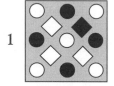

1

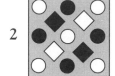

2

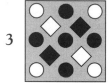

3

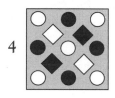

4

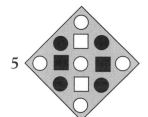

5

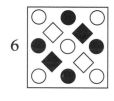

6

19) Complete the following analogy.

  is to   as   is to

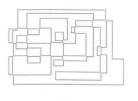

1

2

3

4

20) Which of the numbered figures best completes the series?

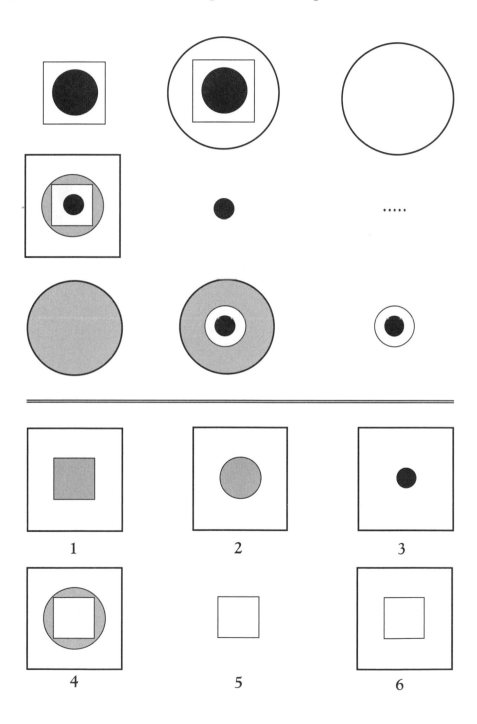

1

2

3

4

5

6

21) Which of the numbered figures best completes the series?

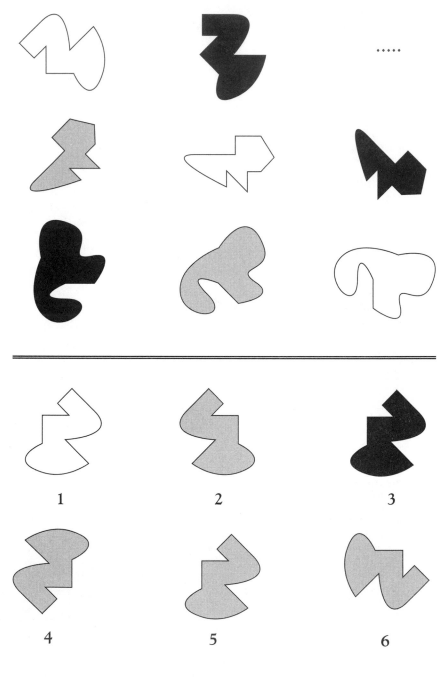

22) Which of the following figures does not belong?

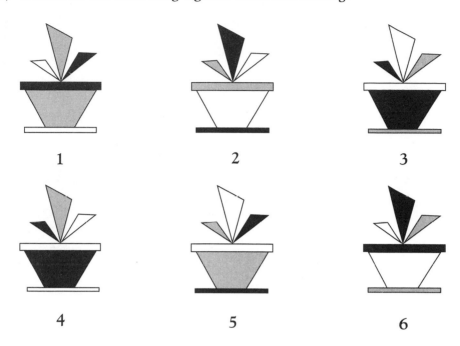

1 2 3

4 5 6

23) Which of the numbered figures comes next in the series?

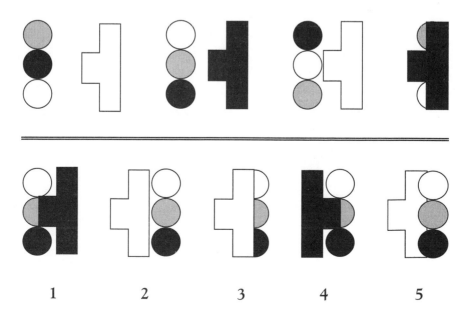

1 2 3 4 5

24) Which of these figures does not belong?

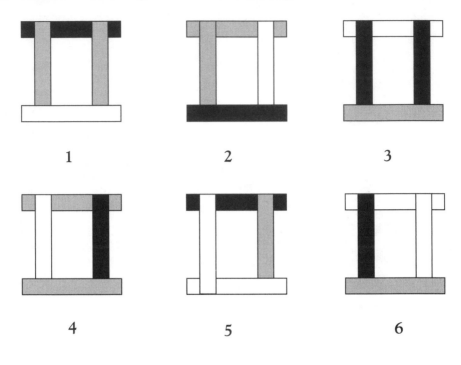

1   2   3

4   5   6

25) Which of these figures does not belong?

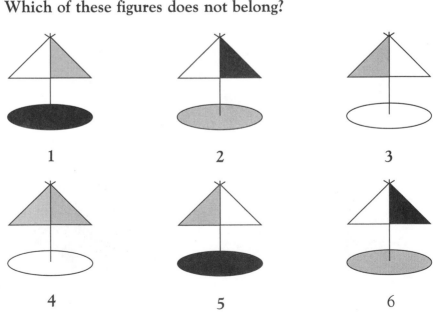

1   2   3

4   5   6

26) Which of these figures does not belong?

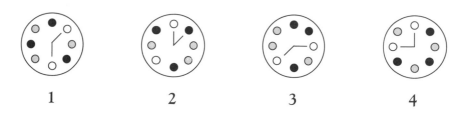

1   2   3   4

27) Which of these figures does not belong?

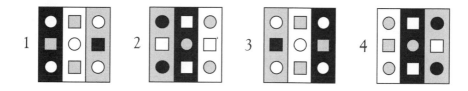

28) Which of the numbered figures comes next in the series?

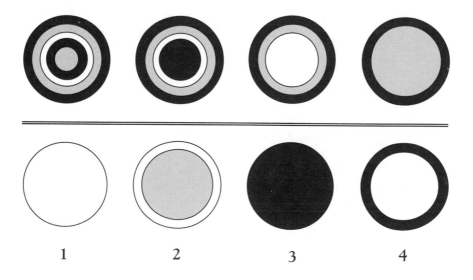

1   2   3   4

29) Which of these figures does not belong?

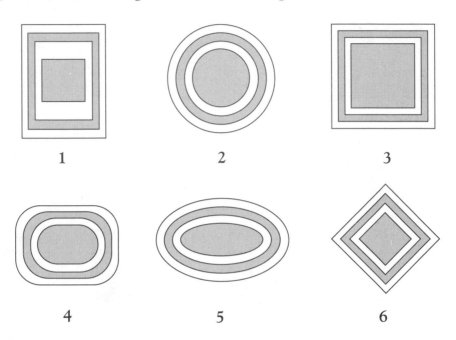

30) Which of the numbered figures comes next in the series?

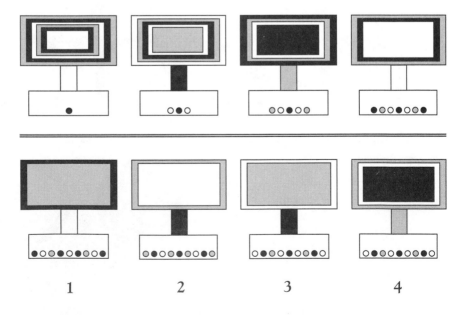

31) Which of these figures does not belong?

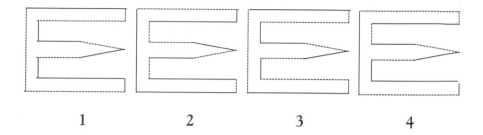

1   2   3   4

32) Which of these figures does not belong?

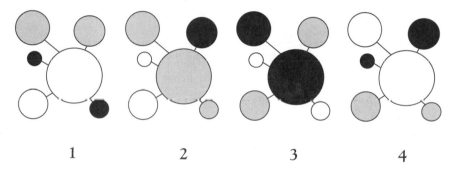

1   2   3   4

For solutions, turn to page 158.

Spatial Test Solutions

1) **2.** Subtract the second figure from the first figure.

2) **5.** The figures approach each other, alternate between black and gray, and alternate between solid and dotted lines.

3) **3.** The white becomes black.

4) **2.** The rhombus becomes a circle and alternates between black and gray. In the inside, the square figures become rhombuses and alternate between black and white.

5) **5.** The first, second, and third vertical columns are in the first dimension.

6) **5.** The figure rotates.

7) **5.** The inside "L" turns in a clockwise direction.

8) **2.** A line is progressively eliminated while remaining lines alternate between solid and dotted.

9) **1.** The figure is upside down, rotates 180°, and changes from gray to black.

10) **3.** The figures overlap.

11) **4.** Each figure alternates between white and gray while the windows and doors remain black.

12) **4.** Every rectangle has 5 black squares, 5 white squares, and 5 gray squares.

13) **3.** Every figure has 5 squares and 4 circles.

14) **5.** The figures rotate.

15) **5.** There are 5 rhombuses in every figure.

16) **1.** The figures approach each other and overlap.

17) **2.** The figure rotates 180° and the squares become circles.

18) **4.** The initial figure rotates 45° while alternating the shades of the inside components.

19) **3.** The figure turns upside down and the lines become gray.

ŋ) **4.** The element is subtracted in each series.

21) 5. The series alternates among white, black, and gray, and rotates 45°.

22) 4. Each figure has 2 black parts, 2 white parts, and 2 gray parts.

23) 3. The figures progressively approach each other while alternating white, black, and gray circles.

24) 5. The vertical shapes on the bottom are in the second dimension.

25) 4. Each figure alternates among white, black, and gray.

26) 2. The lines connect the two white circles.

27) 4. The shading of the rectangles and the circles and squares inside alternate.

28) 3. Progressively take away each inside circle.

29) 1. The center is not concentric.

30) 3. The balls progressively increase by 2. The upper rectangle progressively loses an inside rectangle.

31) 3. Each figure has 6 dotted lines.

32) 2. Each figure has 2 black, white, and gray balls.

SELF-SCORING

Less than 14 =	Poor	–
From 15 to 18 =	Adequate	☆
From 19 to 22 =	Fair	☆
From 23 to 26 =	Good	☆☆☆
From 27 to 32 =	Excellent	☆☆☆☆

Index

Solutions on *italized* pages.